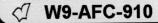
Japanese Schoolgirl Inferno

Tokyo Teen Fashion Subculture Handbook

By Patrick Macias and Izumi Evers

Illustrations by Kazumi Nonaka

CHRONICLE BOOKS
SAN FRANCISCO

Contents

Introduction

Tokyo, Shibuya, Center Street, 2006

We are outside the front gates of a nightclub, nervously wondering if the guy in the ticket booth—who looks like a Barbie doll someone has briefly set on fire, then left out in the rain—will let us inside.

"Hi. We're here researching a book about Japanese schoolgirl culture and fashion. Mind if we come in and take some pictures?"
"Do you have an invitation? This is a private event."
"Uh, no . . ."
"OK, I'll have to check with the people inside."

He vanishes into the club, where a mysterious, unseen force is consulted. A few seconds later, he's back with a nod of affirmation. "Sure. They said it's fine. Go right in."

With the creak of a door, so begins the descent into the dark heart of the Japanese schoolgirl inferno, a world that Dante himself could not have possibly imagined.

Inside the club, there's a circle formed by dozens of high-school-age kids spread around the dance floor. They stand almost shoulder to shoulder, legs apart, performing a dance called "Para Para." Their hands are a blur of quick and elaborate motions, executed in perfect timing to a seizure-inducing Euro-beat soundtrack.

The boys mostly sit in the back, crack jokes, and check their cell phones. The girls (or Gals, as they are commonly known in Japan) lead the dance, and have organized this event down to the last detail. The super-tanned members of the local "Circle"—a grassroots youth organization formed to put on and enjoy group outings—strut about in bleached-blonde hair

and blue eye shadow, wearing matching silk-screened T-shirts that read "Shibuya Para2 Kingdom."

Within a few minutes, the jig is up. We've been discovered hiding in the corner taking notes and generally not fitting in. One of the gals sidles up to us and demands to know what the heck is going on.

"Wow, you guys are doing a book? That's really cool! Sure, you can take my picture! But . . . I'm kinda thirsty. Can I have a drink of your Coke first?"

A bit of refreshment is the very least we owe someone like her. After all, Japanese girls have been tirelessly advancing trends in fashion and cutting-edge culture for decades now. You probably already have an idea of who they are and what they look like. For starters, the image of the Kogal, an innocent yet sexy girl clad in a school uniform with big puffy socks bunched around her ankles, is currently, for better or worse, a

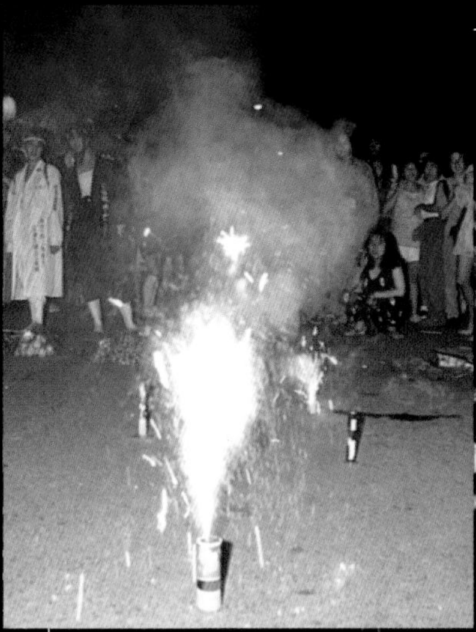

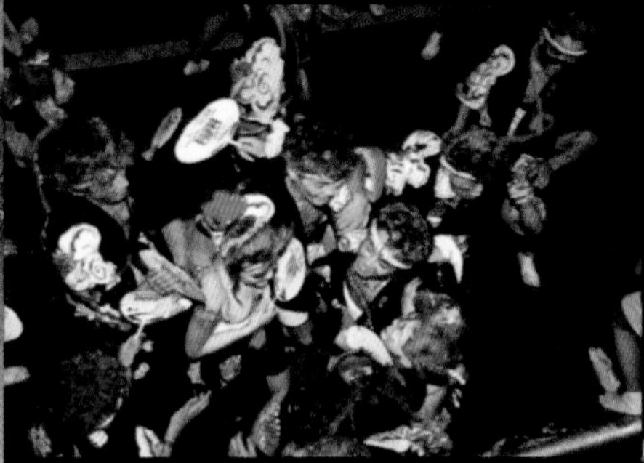

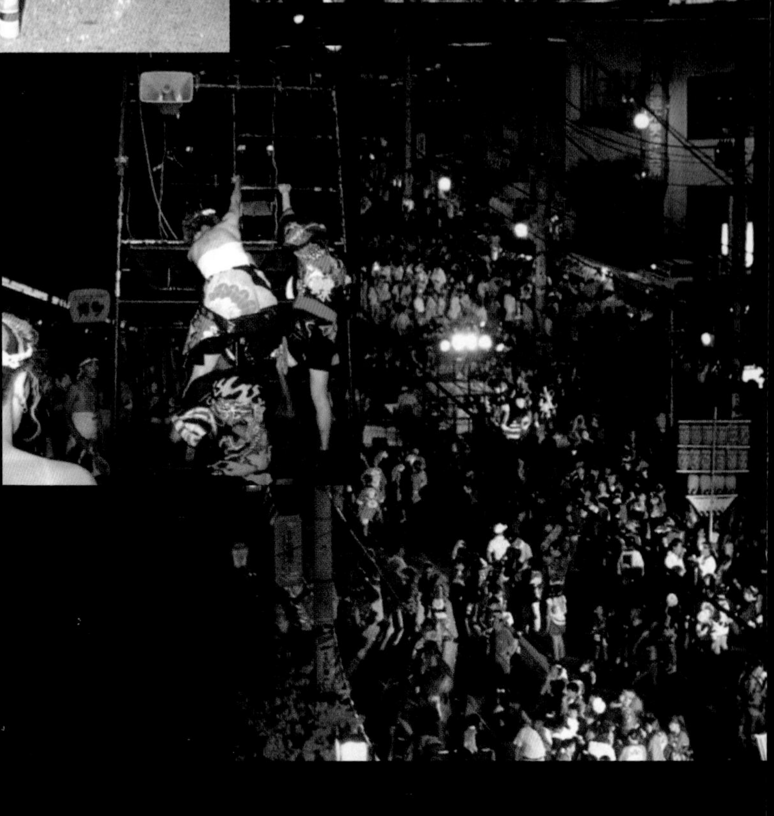

symbol of Japan as much as the kimono-clad geisha and the salaryman in his stuffy business suit.

The murderous character Gogo Yubari helped bring a comic-book version of the Kogal to countless movie screens around the world in *Kill Bill: Vol. 1*. Gwen Stefani warbled on about those "Harajuku Girls" in her 2004 song of the same name. *Wired* magazine even runs a monthly column, "Japanese Schoolgirl Watch," where the latest concerns of these mythic creatures are analyzed in the hopes that they might contain a glimpse of the future. Legendary fashion designer Karl Lagerfeld (Chloé, Chanel, and Fendi) is even said to stop by the Shibuya109 store to keep a close eye on the Gal set's state of the art. But where do the Japanese schoolgirls get their inspiration?

Far too many trends around the world originate from the media,[a] which conspires to ruthlessly plot what we'll be consuming, watching, and wearing for months to come (in a dastardly process known as "preselection"). Meanwhile, many of the Japanese fashion trends documented in this book can be traced to a single person, a girl who created her own unique look all by herself and then took to the streets of Tokyo, inspiring others to follow suit.

What is it about the city of Tokyo in particular that encourages such elaborate fashion and extreme behavior? According to Nobuaki Higa, former editor in chief of *Teen's Road* magazine and a longtime chronicler of youth culture in Japan, "A lot of what you see is rooted in festival (*matsuri*) culture. When you go to a Japanese festival, it's a break with ordinary life. People want to dress up and stand out from the crowd. When you see the dancing and partying done at festivals, it's not all that different from what goes on today."

Tokyo locales such as the Shibuya and Harajuku districts are like a year-round nonstop festival where people can dress up and play roles in a nonstop urban theater.

And Japan is a place where it is easy to form tribes. Says Higa, "Maybe in America you have to overcome a lot of racial and economic barriers

Yet, time and time again, while conducting interviews for this book, we heard a sad refrain from magazine editors, designers, and even the girls on the street themselves. Kei Kawamura, of *Kateigaho International* magazine, a publication for the older set that carefully follows the fashion world, lays out the fundamental problem most succinctly: "Everything has been done already—several times, in fact. It's hard to create something new in the area of fashion."

creativity turns to consumerism. The turnover rate for fads and fashion is astonishingly high. New frontiers must continually be sought.

The boys are catching up fast. Naoki Matsuura, the editor-in-chief of *KERA* magazine, says, "Right now in the fashion industry, people are saying Japanese men's fashion is the most exciting thing going on. Guys are becoming superconscious about their clothes and hairstyles." Take that guy at the door of the nightclub, for example. He's the spitting image of the tanned and bleached Gals dancing inside, which is why his kind is known as a Gal-O (the "O" stands for the Japanese word *otoko*, or "man"). There is even a magazine for guys like him now (an unthinkable concept a few years ago), called *Men's egg*.

After a long run of enjoying their own native fads and fashions, Gals are now eagerly looking outside of Japan for inspiration. When the current generation gets past Beyoncé, Paris Hilton, and Pippi Longstocking, what will they think about the bedazzled and baffled Westerners gazing back at them in shock and awe? Will the result be a fashion flatline, a new trend bound to be short-lived, or the creation of an enduring global Gal culture?

To help kick-start the future, we humbly offer this book as a kind of "greatest hits" of Japanese schoolgirl culture and fashion. Some of the styles on display are "extinct"; others are still going strong. To help tell this decades-spanning saga, we've broken the lot down into three basic categories, encompassing Bad, Sexy, and Arty Gals. Our profiles of each individual type include a style history, must-have items, and even ideal boyfriends. Also included are resources for further reading, viewing, and shopping for those seeking further insight into what makes these girls tick, or just information on where to find a pair of 8-inch-tall platform shoes if you'd like to adopt the look yourself.

The door to the club in Shibuya is still open. Now would be a good time to learn how to Para Para dance.

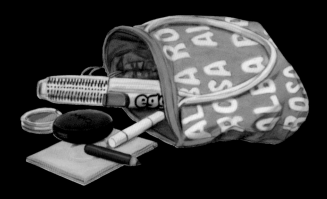

BAD GALS

Mean Streets (Late 1960s to Late 1970s)

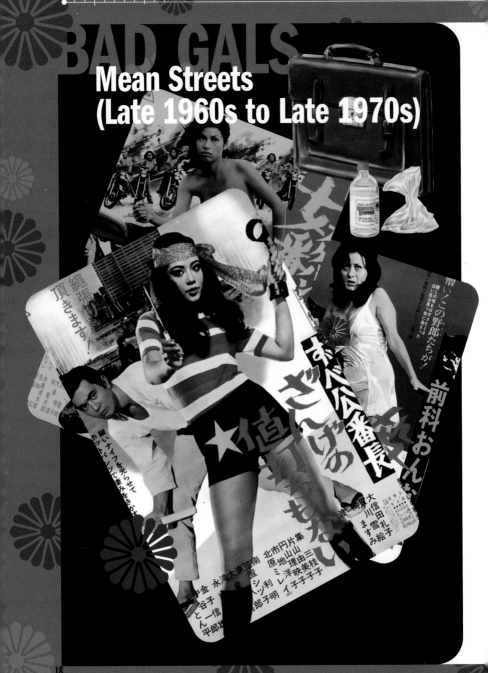

Tokyo, 1972

A pack of tough-looking teenagers sits smoking cigarettes in a huddle near a Japan Railways train station. Everything about them, including their style of speech, is tough as nails. Hands clutch barely concealed weapons, including razors and steel chains, should a fight break out. And it's only a matter of time until one does. Their collective body language bristles with a threat of imminent violence. Local *yakuza* gangsters protecting their turf? Neighborhood bad boys daring straight, polite Japanese society to knock the chip off their shoulders? Well, almost. It's a group of schoolgirls known as the Sukeban, Japan's very first all-girl gangs.

The name comes from the Japanese words for "female" (*suke*) and "boss" (*ban*). Although they enjoyed only a brief vogue in the early 1970s, the Sukeban made for a truly unforgettable social disease: shoplifting, pickpocketing, and rivaling the very worst of the menfolk for misbehavior and outrageous acts of violence.

Why weren't they all rounded up and thrown into the slammer? Says bad-teen historian Nobuaki Higa, "In Japan, outlaw society is right out in the open. Yakuza gangsters can even have their own office buildings. Even though you might be antisocial, that doesn't mean you are unacceptable, especially if you are young. The cops know it's just a matter of time before bad girls will grow up and walk away from the lifestyle. Being in a gang is something you can graduate from."

Today, classic Sukeban fashion, typified by a long, flowing skirt and immense Afro-like hair, is considered woefully out of style. But the Sukeban's way of life—a revolutionary mix of to-the-death sisterhood, ironclad rules, and an underworld-style flair for organization—continues to influence Japanese schoolgirls whenever they gather in packs.

Super Material for the third season of the *Sukeban Dekka (Sukeban Cops)* TV show.

One major aspect of Sukeban style can be seen to this day. Indeed, it is a major contribution to the universally accepted image of the Japanese bad girl. The Sukeban religiously wore their school uniforms, of the *Sailor Fuku* variety (the classic sailor suit the Japanese school system forces female students to wear), no matter what manner of naughty behavior they engaged in. The tradition has stuck with generations of girls since, from the Kogals of the 1990s right up until today's Shibuya District Gals (although the skirts have since gotten a whole lot shorter).

The Sukeban gangs did not appear in a vacuum. When they first began sprouting in Japan during the mid-1960s, the girls took their inspiration from the numerous bad-boy gangs that surrounded them. Male classmates who would have once joined the yakuza were instead beginning to form their own local gangs in a pint-size imitation of the grown-up underworld. Fierce territorial battles with other rival schools and hoods soon resulted.

Such all-male groups and their members were *"Bancho* groups" (the Japanese term for schoolyard boss was *Bancho*). They had power and status, and it was only a matter of time until the girls demanded a piece of the action for themselves.

The first Sukeban gangs probably began with just a few girls sneaking cigarettes in the school bathroom. But within a few years, the ranks of female gangs began to swell and organize with impressive virus-like efficiency.

During the mid-'60s, the gangs ranged in size from Tokyo's United Shoplifters Group, which numbered eighty girls in all, up to the Kanto

Women Delinquent Alliance, the single biggest Sukeban organization, made up of some twenty thousand girls from across western Japan. Like a real corporate entity, the alliance boasted within its ranks a president, an adviser, and even an accountant.

The Sukeban phenomenon peaked in 1972 with the emergence of the single most fearsome Sukeban in history. Hailing from the Tokyo suburbs of Saitama, K-Ko the Razor commanded a private army of fifty women warriors. Her nickname came from her weapon of choice: a razor tightly wrapped in cloth and tucked between her breasts, whipped out with superhuman speed to slash her enemies' faces.

Few Sukeban cast quite as menacing a shadow as did K-Ko, whose exploits became an urban legend of sorts, but physical violence of one sort or another was an everyday fact of life for many. Not only were there plenty of rival factions to tangle with, but there was also ample opportunity to inflict damage on members of one's own gang. Breaking the rules (and the Sukeban loved to make rules) could result in a physical sanction known as "lynching."

Lynching involved several degrees of punishment, beginning with a lit cigarette applied to bare skin, which was considered getting off easy. The same cigarette applied to more-intimate parts of the body ranked as "medium." The harshest of punishments rival anything in the annals of the Spanish Inquisition and are simply too terrible to mention here.

Reasons for lynching were numerous and differed from gang to gang. They might include showing disrespect to the senior members, speaking to "enemies," or being caught doing drugs (although sniffing paint thinner for a quick and cheap high was common among Sukeban and, indeed, among bad girls and boys everywhere).

The most common cause of a lynching was fooling around with the opposite sex. Cheating on a boyfriend (inevitably a bad boy or a Bancho gang member himself) would surely lead to a lynching—that is, if a member even bothered with guys in the first place. Because of the emotional nature of the relationships between the girl-gang members, jealously and crushes on other members could lead to intense, soap-opera-style drama.

In spite of all the petty crimes the Sukeban casually indulged in, the girls themselves were convinced that they were living by high moral standards. Perhaps the chasteness of the Sukeban (take those long skirts, for instance) was a reaction to the permissiveness of the sexual revolution of the 1960s. Dressing sexy and wearing too much makeup were frowned upon. These were girls who wanted to look and act tougher and older than they actually were. But the chain- and razor-packing Sukeban were surprisingly conservative when it came to matters of dating and romance.

You wouldn't think so based on the "Sukeban" films churned out by the exploitation-minded Toei Studios. Full of nudity and *Switchblade Sisters* girl-gang mayhem, the movies probably said more about the fantasies of male audiences and filmmakers than they did about the lives of the girls themselves. Still, the films are a heck of a lot of fun.

Even as the actual Sukeban gangs began to decline in numbers, their myths continue to endure in pop culture. The long-running *Be Bop High School* comic books, animation, and live-action films and television shows serve up comedic bad-boy and bad-girl action for the masses. There is also the *Sukeban Dekka* (*Sukeban Cops*) franchise, which depicts undercover teenage policewomen in sailor suits fighting crime with razor-sharp origami cranes and yo-yos.

But the actual Sukeban phenomenon itself had gone on the skids by the mid-1970s. Gang members were growing up, graduating from "the life," or slowly becoming integrated into society. And the next generation of teenagers would soon be dancing in the streets instead of just sitting in them. ✿

Profile:

SuKeBaN

FACE CHECK!
Super-thin eyebrows

Razor

Customized embroidered school uniform

Chain weapon

Sailor-style school uniform

School slippers

Long school skirt

23

Ideal Boyfriend

Must Items

Razor

Small, easy to conceal, and good for making scars that last a lifetime.

Highs

Need a cheap high? A plastic bag of paint thinner will do in a pinch. Just don't start crying if your teeth melt and your liver gives out.

Wimps need not apply. You want a *tough guy* who lives by a code of honor.

Bamboo Sword

"Borrowed" from the school gym. Good for keeping trouble at bay or starting some yourself.

Flat School Bag

How to make your bag extremely thin (thinner is better): boil it in water.

Cigarettes

The most popular brands were Lark, Mild Seven, and Hope.

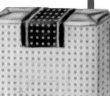

SUKEBAN

BAD GALS

Dance, Dance, Revolution (Late 1970s to Early 1980s)

Tokyo, Harajuku, Summer of 1979

It's a street, a big one, but no vehicle—save perhaps a Sherman tank–could hope to pass through it. And yet the area is plagued by a traffic jam—a human one. Thousands of kids clad in garishly colored, shiny robes are dancing in packs with unnerving, robotlike precision. Like many youth gatherings before and since, the mood is faintly reminiscent of a religious festival. But this is no holiday. It's just another weekend in Pedestrian Heaven (*hokosha tengoku*), a part of town under occupation by a mass of street dancers known as the Takenokozoku (Bamboo Sprout Tribe).

The teenage girls within the ranks far outnumber the boys, and they were the first kids to reinvent Tokyo's Harajuku District as a haven for street culture and delirious fashion. Takenokozoku girls covered themselves in cheap accessories like plastic whistles, beads, and stuffed animals purchased in neighborhood stores, a look that anticipated the Decora look of decades later. Local boutiques and designers inspired the clothes they wore, but the girls often opted to make their own outfits, much like today's Gothloli. Most of these kids came from the suburbs, but history still owes them a debt as the very first Harajuku Girls.

Decades later, tourists eager to gaze upon today's oddly-garbed Gals in their natural environment must endure crowded sidewalks and climb traffic overpasses for a glimpse of what amounts to maybe thirty costumed kids on a good day. But during the brief but memorable heyday of the street dancers, a half-mile-long stretch of road behind Harajuku's Yoyogi Park prohibited traffic on the street—hence, the area's nickname of Pedestrian Heaven. The Takenokozoku didn't go there just to hang out. These girls came to dance, dance, dance.

Beginning in 1978, kids who were too young (or too cheap) to go to a disco began invading Pedestrian Heaven with a bevy of boom boxes. An epic outdoor party ensued. At the peak of the craze, in the summer of 1979, some five thousand kids on average were gathering weekly to perform their choreographed dance in the street. The giant crowds broke down into individual groups–which included the Runners, Rainbow and Elegance, Utopia, Angels, and Friends–who identified themselves with giant banners and group names stitched into clothing.

The Takenokozoku weren't bad in the same antisocial sense as the Sukeban girl gangs, but a comparison to a plague of locusts would not be totally off the mark. The most delinquent behavior they indulged in was stealing advertising banners from suburban stores in the middle of the night. The banners were then worn as capes, resulting in a lot of girls who seemed to be selling used cars.

The cult took its name and style from a Harajuku designer boutique called Takenoko (Baby Bamboo), which opened in 1978. The store sold baggy clothes inspired by traditional Japanese dress, such as kimonos from the Heian era (AD 794 to 1185). Takenoko's brand-name goods were expensive, so the kids in the Chiba and Saitama suburbs tried to re-create the look as best they could, by whatever means necessary. The results were more MC Hammer than Old World chic.

Takenokozoku draped themselves in loose-fitting outfits, usually polyester robes bright enough to attract hummingbirds (hot pink, purple, blue, and violet) and decorated with kanji characters. Underneath, they sported baggy pants; their dancin' feet were typically clad in cozy school slippers and kung-fu shoes.

More than anything, Takenokozoku girls looked like little kids playing dress-up. Their favored accessories included oversize lace ribbons; long, fake pearl necklaces; paper hats; and, for that extra touch of elementary-school style, "Hi! My Name Is . . " name-tag stickers. Such ensemble outfits may not have aged well, but the Takenokozoku style was still a major breakthrough in Japanese street fashion in one key respect: it owed nothing to Western influences.

Previously, the foreigner-friendly Harajuku District had been the haunt of young Japanese adults who worshipped 1950s-style American rock and roll, clad in Levi's and secondhand clothes that once belonged to U.S. families living in military housing. The rockers prided themselves on their careful attention to detail and decades-spanning knowledge of foreign music and pop culture.

But the upstart Takenokozoku cared little about . . . well, anything, really. They just wanted to *party*. Inevitably, that meant choreographed group dancing in the streets.

The steps themselves bore a resemblance to traditional Odori dancing done at seasonal religious festivals in Japan (in fact, Pedestrian Heaven was just a stone's throw away from a Shinto temple). Odori would also seem to be an ancestor of the Para Para dancing that many of today's teenage Gals devote their lives to.

The dance was kind of an unhurried hand jive, the Hokey Pokey with most of the action confined to the upper body. Busting out with unique and individual expressive moves was not valued in the slightest. The basic goal of Takenokozoku dancing was to dance it in perfect formation along with everybody else. The phenomenon might seem to speak volumes about the importance of conformity in Japanese society, but, then again, Western line dancing isn't much different.

Despite having lugged massive boom boxes all the way from the suburbs, the Takenokozoku cared little about the selection of music. Whatever was on the top of the pops that day (mostly now-obscure candy pop, disco from Europe, and top-selling singles) was good enough; be it Arabesque, Dschinghis Khan, the Nolan Sisters, the Dooleys, ABBA, or the Electric Light Orchestra, it would do just fine for the synchronized communal dance.

Naturally, the music-connoisseur rock 'n' rollers hated them with a passion, leading to fierce fighting. Boys could expect knuckle sandwiches, while the girls would endure cries of "Go back to the countryside! You are not from Tokyo!" from a bunch of greaseballs studiously dressed like Elvis.

The media quickly fell in love with the cheerful, colorful Takenokozoku. The summer of 1979 saw the kids not just dancing in the street but on television sets nationwide. The first Takenokozoku celebrity was minted when dancer Hiroyuki Okita was plucked out of Pedestrian Heaven by a big-time talent agency to become a pop star and television actor. But this proved to be a fatal blow to the scene, as fame-lusting wannabes of all ages soon overwhelmed Harajuku. The Takenokozoku, lacking any deep philosophical commitment to maintaining their culture, cashed in their chips pretty quick. Many switched over to the Next Big Thing: a regrettable Westernized style known as American Casual (think tennis visors, roller skates, and cardigans). Still, a distant echo of the Takenokozoku influence appears in the air whenever packs of kids gather to hang out in Harajuku. And those human dancing machines even wound up showing the rockers a thing or two.

After the Takenokozoku split, the Elvis clones took over Pedestrian Heaven and proceeded to do the Peppermint Twist in the street with all their might. In the 1990s, during an era known as the "band boom," the area became a haven for live music and remained that way until the traffic came back in 1998, and the gates of Pedestrian Heaven were finally nailed shut. ★

Profile:

TAKENOKO ZOKU

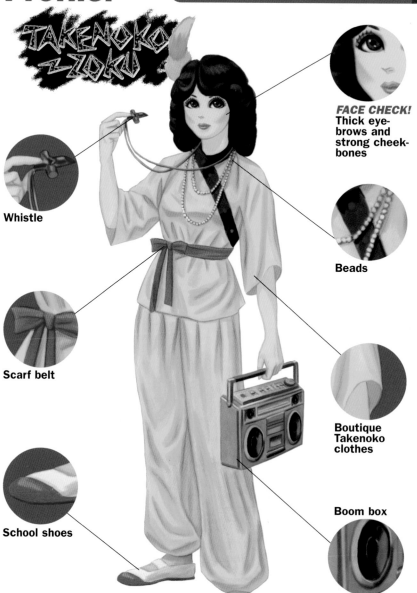

FACE CHECK!
Thick eye-
brows and
strong cheek-
bones

Whistle

Beads

Scarf belt

**Boutique
Takenoko
clothes**

School shoes

Boom box

Ideal Boyfriend

Must Items

Beads
Bright and eye-catching.

Whistle
Blow it in time to the rhythm.

Macho men need not apply. Takenokozoku gals want a guy who can hold his own in sickly shades of pink, purple, and violet. Must be a good dancer and able to protect his sweetie from peepers while she changes outfits in the park.

Kung-Fu Shoes or School Slippers
Your feet will thank you.

Baggy Clothes and *Happi* Coat

Inspired by the traditional Japanese fashions found at Takenoko boutique.

Name Tag

In case you should ever forget who you are.

Boom Box

To play cassette tapes of all the latest hits, regardless of what they are.

Ribbon

A big one, like something out of a 1950s sock hop.

Speed Tribes
(Mid-1980s to Mid-1990s)

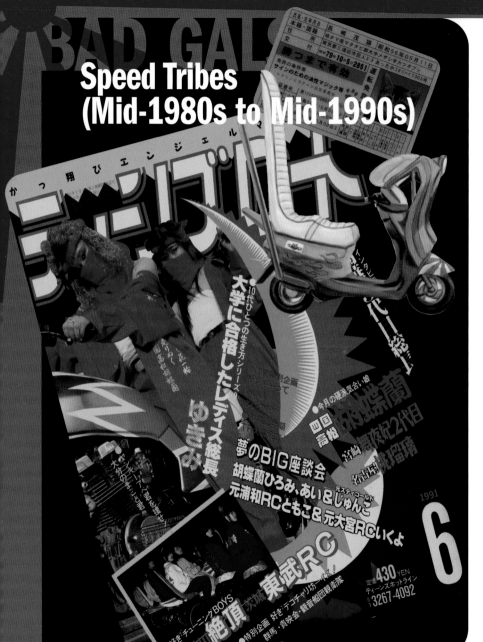

Tokyo, Shinjuku, 1991

Somewhere between question and answer, conducting an interview for the magazine *Teen's Road* in the streets of Tokyo, journalist Ryo Tochinai found himself in the middle of a gang war. He was slashed in the leg with a razor, while others nearby got it in the face. The berserker who started the trouble was a member of a biker gang, an all-girl biker gang. But they prefer to be called Lady's.

Japanese kids and motorcycles have an epic love affair stretching back to the late 1950s, when James Dean and Marlon Brando movies inspired the first generation of what the media dubbed "Thunder Tribes" and, later, "Speed Tribes" (*Bosozoku*).

The Hell's Angels–styled boys-only gangs that they formed included such legendary tribes as Specter, Mad Special, Alley Cats, and Black Emperor. From the mid-1960s on, they gathered in a group of up to one thousand strong for noisy nightly rides through Tokyo's Shinjuku District. These born-to-lose troublemakers popped methamphetamine pills and sniffed massive amounts of paint thinner as they revved up their hot steel hogs. Predictably, motorcycle-related fatality rates in Japan rose 60 percent by the late sixties.

By the early 1970s, the girlfriends and groupies of these "crazy riders" began to form their own organizations. But these gangs, such as Specter Lady's and Mad Special Lady's, were regarded as supporters or, worse, mere mascots of the much bigger all-male packs.

The Speed Tribes were a force to be reckoned with. Police estimated that there were some 817 separate gangs in all and that twenty-six thousand boys and girls were involved in the biker lifestyle in one way or another (unofficial headcounts placed the figures three times as high). And as the media became infatuated by the biker phenomenon, the numbers would only multiply.

In 1975 all-out gang warfare erupted between factions all over Japan. By 1977 not a day went by without reports in the newspaper of the latest rumble and the police's increasingly helpless attempts to maintain order. In 1978 the Japanese government criminalized riding together in groups, slapping the cuffs on the golden age of the male-dominated biker gangs.

Then a funny thing started to happen. While the boys began to hang up their leather jackets and put the pomade back in the cupboard, the numbers of female motorcycle gangs in Tokyo actually began to increase. They cast away their affiliations with the old groups like Specter and began to form all-new biker gangs. Collectively, they were known as Lady's and were created, as one member put it, "by girls, for girls." Baby Face, Team Popeye, and Evil Girls were among these new gangs that quickly claimed the streets.

A new magazine called *Teen's Road,* catering especially to Lady's, debuted in 1989. It featured glossy color photos of biker parties, profiles of cute boys (Lady's bosses tended to prefer slightly feminine, weaker men), and success stories of Lady's who'd gotten jobs in bars or given birth. *Teen's Road* brought the female biker style and fashion to the suburbs, where it proved a massive hit with the terminally bored girls who lived there.

The Year of the Lady's came in 1991. *Teen's Road* editor Nobuaki Higa estimates that there were three hundred different groups in all and that more than ten thousand Lady's were racing through the streets of cities and suburbs alike on choppers made mostly by Honda and Kawasaki.

The basic attitude and structure of the Lady's gangs were derived from the Sukeban juvenile delinquents of a decade before. Like them, members often indulged in drugs and petty crime but also lived by a seemingly contradictory set of ethics and moral codes. Bonds between members were intense and were based on the *kohai-sempai* (pupil-mentor) system found throughout Japanese society. And when they weren't riding around on customized bikes with their blaring "Ahoogah" horns, the Lady's were practicing what anthropologists call "rites of passage." For instance, when members reached the age of eighteen, a festive and tear-stained "graduation" ceremony was held. Gangs also offered plenty of emotional support, just like a surrogate family.

Girl biker fashion evolved largely from the Takenokozoku, which seemed like a natural since some suburban Lady's gangs were originally formed by former street dancers. The Lady's abandoned the black-leather gear of the boys' gangs for loose, one-color robes called *Tokko fuku,* just like the Takenokozoku used to wear.

These garments would then be covered in elaborate, hand-stitched calligraphic lettering that stressed either gang affiliation or hard-ass slogans of the "live fast, die young" variety. Underneath the robe, where a bra might have been, was the traditional tightly wrapped band of white cloth known as a *sarashi,* while a white sweatband on the forehead would double as a halo of sorts. The result was a uniquely Japanese look, somewhere between a sushi chef and a patriotic auto mechanic.

Like the girl gangs of the 1970s, the Lady's began to form regional alliances, including *Sukeren* (Women's Federation), which numbered one thousand members in all—most of whom had long criminal records (new members were not allowed to join if they were scared of going to jail). Another Lady's supergang was the Killer Federation, led by a mythic criminal mastermind named Noriko, who is said to have relocated to California to avoid capture by the cops.

As *Teen's Road* continued to popularize the Lady's movement, the magazine was flying off the shelves to the tune of twenty thousand copies a month. But the success had an unintended side effect: the original biker aesthetic was beginning to get watered down. Soon there were Lady's who didn't ride motorcycles at all and formed "gangs" just to try to get their pictures printed; these poseurs were pejoratively referred to as Mass Commi (Mass Communications) Lady's. The hard-core girls began to tell *Teen's Road* reporters, "Don't call us Lady's anymore. Call us Female Hoodlums (*onna gokudo*) instead!"

Teen's Road ceased publication in 1992. As former editor-in-chief Higa explains, "The staff was tired of being physically assaulted by the readers." Some of the Lady's themselves were fleeing the scene for similar reasons. A wave of bad mojo was blowing in from the male-dominated Japanese underworld. Some Lady's were being kidnapped and forced into prostitution.

But the combination of motorcycles and speed-crazy Japanese kids continues to endure. Although Tokyo streets are now relatively safe from drug-addled dropout bikers, the suburbs (where traffic laws are less likely to be enforced) are still menaced by low-life motorists known as *Yanki*. (According to legend, since the first generation of Yanki had a fondness for tacky American clothes like Hawaiian shirts, they got the name from the ever-popular slogan "Yankee, go home.") Bikes don't always figure into the lifestyle. Some Yanki group activities are confined to merely squatting around smoking cigarettes in the parking lot of a convenience store, mostly because there's not much else to do out there in the middle of nowhere.

Set in the sleepy town of Shimotsuma, the movie *Kamikaze Girls* depicts an unlikely friendship between two Japanese schoolgirl archetypes: a Yanki and a Lolita. In the film, the hellcat Yanki, played to perfection by actress Anna Tsuchiya, is depicted as a holdover from a different era. Indeed, today, with the bad kids looking to hip-hop for inspiration, Yanki are considered laughably uncool.

It might seem like the end is nigh for both the Yanki and the Japanese biker-girl tradition in general, but hope springs eternal. As long as Japan has countryside and young women who are bored out of their minds, someone is going to want to escape by whatever means necessary. Hopefully, the clutch of a Honda or a Kawasaki will be within reach. ✳

(Left) A Lady's meeting is held between bosses (standing) and members (seated) somewhere in the suburbs of Japan.

(Below) A cute little *Nameneko* kitten.

Q and A

During the early 1990s, Takako was a member of Evil Girls (*Akujo*), a Tokyo-based Lady's biker gang. Now, she is a licensed kindergarten teacher (rare, as most of her peers never graduated from high school) and works in the Shinjuku District.

Q: How did you wind up joining the Evil Girls gang?

A: I was in middle school, and my *sempai* (elder classmate) was getting into the Lady's scene. It just seemed so cool.

Q: What sort of bike did you ride?

A: It was a Honda-CBR 400cc. It was white with a thunder seat. There was a place to put the gang's flag in the back, but it was never used. There was always someone holding it.

Q: What were some of the best things about being a member of the gang?

A: Everything, really. I learned a lot about people and human relationships. There were one thousand of us, and it just felt so incredible to gather and ride in a big group like that. You felt really strong and unstoppable. It was even fun when the cops chased us. They used to ask us things like "Would you do this again in your next life?" but I think they were trying to look after us and protect us. Sometimes we'd even go out for dinner together.

Q: What were some of the bad things that happened?

A: Things really changed when the Chinese Mafia began moving in. It began to get violent and dangerous. One of my friends was kidnapped by a *chimpira* (low-ranked yakuza), who sold her into prostitution. We wanted to get revenge and save her, but that would have been suicide. I really feel bad about that even today.

Q: If someone wanted to join your gang, what was the most important quality she had to have?

A: Guts. Once, a girl came to us and said she was going to take us all on in a fight by herself. That was really impressive, so we wound up recruiting her. ✳

Profile:

Lady's

FACE CHECK!
Purple eye shadow

Cigarettes

Embroidery

***Sarashi* cloth**

***Tokko fuku* coat**

Net sandals

Motorbike helmet

43

Ideal Boyfriend

Must Items

Tokko Fuku Robe

The more slogans and designs you have, the higher your status in the gang.

Ami (Net) Sandals

Ride the "Crazy Thunder Road" in total comfort. Black pumps were popular footwear, too.

A tough guy who doesn't mind taking orders from his "Lady" from time to time.

Gauze Mask

Makes you look a bit scary. The inside can also be lined with paint thinner in the name of "one for the road."

Nameneko Goods

Photos of cute little kittens dressed up as biker gang members and smoking in the bathroom, generally being bad.

Bike

Just like the big bad *Bosozoku* bikers had. The Lady's also rode customized scooters.

Lady's

School Uniforms

Imagine being forced to wear the same darn thing every day to school, being trapped in the same cut of fabric as everyone around you. By all rights, this is what the history of the Japanese school uniform should be: a dull study in conformity.

And yet, the blazer and skirt ensemble that makes up the modern middle school and high school uniform in Japan is far from a fashion dead end. Not only do Japanese girls get to have fun ingeniously customizing their own uniforms, but big-name fashion designers have also gotten into the act of designing them.

Things have come a long way since the late 19th century, when Japan's mad race for modernization made the wearing of Western-style school uniforms compulsory. In 1921, the now-classic sailor uniform (or sailor *fuku*) made its debut. Modeled after clothes worn by the British Royal Navy, it resulted in decades of Japanese girls who resembled that kid on the front of the Cracker Jack box.

By the time the 1980s rolled around, private schools had begun switching to blazer-jacket-and-skirt-style uniforms. Public schools soon followed their example. But there was another reason for the move away from the sailor suit besides the mere march of time. Declining birthrates in Japan meant that money-starved schools had to come up with fresh ways to lure new students in their doors. The lack of old-fashioned naval gear, just like mom used to wear, seemed to help.

In the 1990s, the blazer uniforms became downright cool to wear even 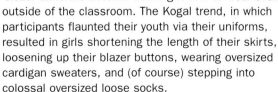 outside of the classroom. The Kogal trend, in which participants flaunted their youth via their uniforms, resulted in girls shortening the length of their skirts, loosening up their blazer buttons, wearing oversized cardigan sweaters, and (of course) stepping into colossal oversized loose socks.

Since school uniforms were going through a street fashion renaissance, uniform manufacturers (most of

them based in the Okayama Prefecture) began contracting with major designers to create new clothes for use in schools. Some of the high-profile brands that were contracted to concoct uniforms include such names as Benetton, Comme Ça du Mode, Hiromichi Nakano, and ELLE. Other cutting-edge Japanese fashion labels, like Lovers Rock, began to design clothes that closely resembled school uniforms, albeit with punk rock touches like safety pins and the old skull-and-crossbones logo.

But not everyone has been won over by the school uniform's move into modern fashion. Graduates complained that changing the style of the uniform every couple of years, as was the new custom thanks to contracts with the design brands, created a break with school history. And not all students were impressed, either. Some girls preferred the classic boring old uniform instead of something thought to be more "original" by a bunch of conniving grown-ups. Most of the fun in having a uniform, it seems, comes from personalizing the clothes yourself rather than letting a fashion designer do it all for you. A sort of compromise has been reached via a new experimental "mix and match" system that some schools are using. Students can go to the school's Web site and choose from a selection of basic designs and fabrics to make their own pre-fab customized uniform.

But the uniform itself is only the tip of the iceberg. There are also massive school uniform "encyclopedia" books that catalog all known varieties and variations, companies that manufacture limited-edition miniature uniform replicas for dolls, and a thriving second-hand market for rare uniforms (which are sometimes purchased by male collectors known as "uniform fans"). The result is that the modern school uniform has become as celebrated in Japan as the classic kimono.

Don't you wish you were forced to wear one now?

SEXY GALS

Socks Life
(Mid- to Late 1990s)

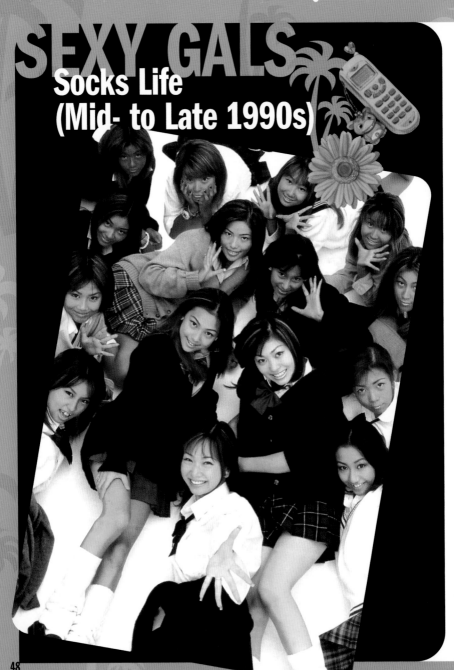

Tokyo, Shibuya, 1996

"The old man is nothing but a purse."

When these words—spoken by an eighth-grade girl who made $4,000 a month "dating" middle-aged men for profit—were printed in a 1996 issue of *Gendai Weekly* magazine, they scandalized the nation of Japan. The media dubbed this young, amoral, wanton creature, who had seemingly been beamed down from the planet Greed but made Tokyo's Shibuya District her home away from home, a "Kogal."

The term *Gal* had been in circulation in Japan since the eighties and now is used to describe young women who simply dress trendy and sexy. The word *Ko* comes from the word *kodomo* (child). While previous Japanese schoolgirl tribes, such as the Sukeban and Lady's, tried to break from societal norms by acting tougher and older than they actually were, the Kogals went in the opposite direction. They flaunted their youth (the class uniform functioned as a kind of badge of authenticity of school age) and wanted to look as adorable as humanly possible. To that end, they spent copious amounts of cash on Hello Kitty accessories, stickers, stuffed animals, and hair ornaments.

Kogals had dark, artificially tanned skin, the result of frequent trips to the tanning salon. They also favored colossal platform boots, bleached hair, and short skirts. The look was, in part, a holdover from an earlier "L.A. Casual" trend in which Japanese kids, adrift in the concrete jungle of Shibuya, were suddenly convinced they were actually a bunch of surfers and beach bunnies.

The loose socks associated with Japanese teen girl fashion were originally created to fit inside oversize rain boots. Some fashion historians who have tried to trace the exact starting point of the trend believe they first came from a manufacturing plant in Sendai in the Miyagi prefecture, while others credit Mito City in Ibaragi. As girls demanded increasingly over-the-top styles and sizes, makers stepped up to the plate by offering wares up to two meters long. Why hide one's lower extremities inside a big puffy white cloud? Some Kogals were insecure about the shape of their chubby legs, so loose socks acted as a sort of camouflage. But, more importantly, they just looked cute.

Kogals also loved higher-ticket items such as Burberry scarves and Vuitton handbags, which were available at numerous boutiques in Tokyo's Shibuya District. But such fare cost serious yen, the likes of which even Mom and Dad or a part-time job could not provide.

In the early 1990s, Shibuya, a transportation and trend-driven entertainment hub just down the street from Harajuku, had become home to a new kind of bad boy, known as Teamers because they roved about, often by car, in "teams." They were gangs of hip-hop-addled kids who engaged in *oyaji gari* (old-man hunting), which involved tracking down weak-looking salarymen and then mugging them for their hard-earned cash (the bitter irony being that many Teamers were actually rich kids who didn't need the bread).

The Teamers brought a new kind of dog-eat-dog mentality to the Tokyo streets, and the Japanese schoolgirls (some of whom were dating Teamers) who came to Shibuya to hang out with their friends began to sense an opportunity to make some easy money.

The resulting scam was called *enjo kosai* (paid dating), the Kogal version of old-man hunting. The goal was to find a mark, typically a lonely adult male with lots of money, and then take him for all he was worth. Hopefully, it stopped after a "date" (i.e., a nice dinner and a shopping spree), but sex could, and sometimes did, factor into the deal.

When the scandal of paid dating hit, the Tokyo Metropolitan Government conducted a survey of Japanese schoolgirls from eighth-graders to high school seniors to uncover how widespread the phenomenon actually was. Of the girls who responded, 3.8 percent of the middle school students and 4 percent of the high school students admitted to practicing paid dating at least once. Clearly, not every girl who wandered into Shibuya wearing loose socks and a school uniform was deep in a sordid world of paid dating, but you wouldn't know that from the image that the media projected.

A plethora of Kogal movies (such as *Love and Pop* and *Bounce: Ko-Gals*) and TV dramas were released in quick succession. Meanwhile, newspapers and magazines began reporting scandalous tales from the paid-dating front, which had spread all over Japan—thanks in no small part to newspapers and magazines—with numbing regularity over the next few years.

One such example was the case of "MR X," age forty-six, who was arrested in Chiba in 1999 for handing over 20,000 yen (around $200) to a fifteen-year-old ninth-grader and then taking her to a love hotel (a building full of tacky private rooms designed for romantic trysts, available for short-term rental or overnight stays). If that wasn't bad enough, MR X

egg'S HIGH SCHOOL STYLE REVOLUTION

Pages from the first golden age of *egg* magazine, including a feature where the contents of girls' handbags are carefully scrutinized (lower right).

turned out to be an employee at an Economic Planning Agency somewhere in Chiba (he was transferred after his arrest).

Intellectuals, too, were having a field day with the Kogals. A paper from Chuo University deduced that the subculture was the result of several societal factors—including "a change of ethics, lack of morality, desire for wealth, and loneliness"—that had infected the nation's young. Perhaps it was a side effect of growing up in the 1980s during Japan's bubble economy, when real estate prices and unimaginable material indulgence were at an all-time high. (Whatever happened to "Girls Just Want to Have Fun"?)

In many ways, Kogals were the spirit of the age, and not always in the negative sense. They made the most out of the technology-driven modern world that they lived in and were among the first and most enthusiastic cell-phone users in Japan. They even invented their own language, known as *Galgo,* typing out coded messages to each other with superhuman dexterity of the thumb (e.g., *cho beri ba* meant "really very bad"; *O-ru* meant "staying out 'all night' at a club"). Now, some ten years after the Kogals began making national headlines, nearly everyone in Japan has picked up their pioneering cell-phone habits, if not their fashion sense.

Meanwhile, just as society had them under a microscope, the actual Kogals were moving on. Many were simply growing up and beginning to enter college and the workforce. Others discovered that their deep-tanned looks were driving away boys their own age. A few were even scared straight by violent "Kogal cleansing campaigns" begun by the Japanese underworld, who worried that the concept of paid dating was cutting into their prostitution rackets. Schools, too, struck back by banning loose socks on campus.

Another death knell for the Kogal came in 1999, as the cosmetics industry began pushing the new "white-face look" as a surefire way to obtain lasting human happiness. Trends and styles may change, but the cute and crass spirit of the Kogal continues to haunt the streets of Shibuya and, indeed, wherever brand-name goods and colorful accessories are desired at any cost. 🐾

Profile:

Kogal

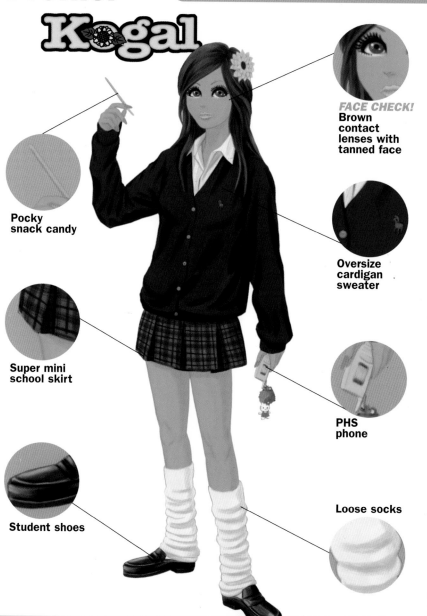

Pocky
snack candy

FACE CHECK!
Brown
contact
lenses with
tanned face

Oversize
cardigan
sweater

Super mini
school skirt

PHS
phone

Student shoes

Loose socks

Ideal Boyfriend

Must Items

Purikura Journal

Purikura (or "print club") photo booths are usually found in video arcades. Take pictures with your pals, snatch up the resulting stickers, and collect them in photo books.

Loose Socks

Nearly always white and very long, usually worn below the knee.

A rich adult male secretly looking for a Kogal girlfriend.

Artificial Flower

As skin tanning became popular, this tropical-style accessory became a huge hit.

Sock Touch

"Socks glue" designed to make the top edge of a sock stick in place.

Pocky

Skinny breadstick dipped in chocolate, strawberry, or other sweet flavorings.

PHS

Even before the modern cell phone, Kogals used these cheap low-range "Personal Handy-phone System" devices to talk to each other within a limited distance. The Kogal's interest in mobile phone technology helped to spread the use of cell phones across Japan. Before the PHS, pagers were used to send number-coded messages, most based on the various ways numbers could be read in Japanese. Some codes, such as 4649 (Yo-ro-si-ku: literally, "nice to meet you" or "hello") and 3341 (Sa-mi-shi-i: "I feel lonely"), still persist in mobile message lingo today.

SEXY GALS

Black Power
(Late 1990s to Early 2000s)

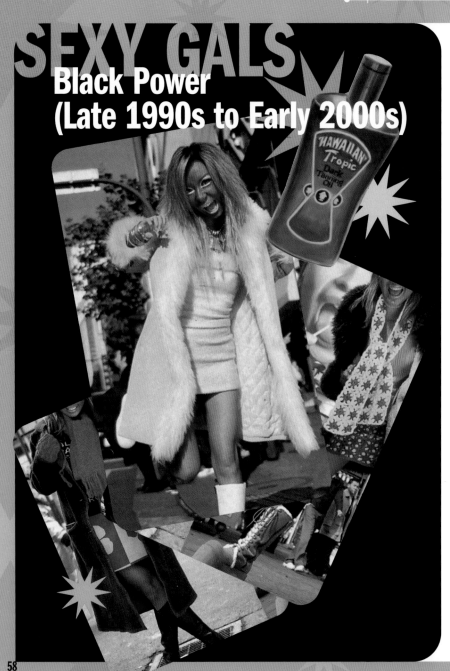

Tokyo, Shibuya, 2000

The girls are in blackface. There's no other way to describe it. They've drastically darkened the color of their once-fair skin through frequent trips to the tanning salon, piling on cheap tanning products from the drugstore, or, in a pinch, applying good old-fashioned shoe polish. White circles that surround their mouths and eyes (made with concealer) heighten the effect: a shocking hybrid between a human being and a panda bear. Then there is the hair, dyed bizarre shades along the orange-to-blonde spectrum or tinted silver gray for a style known as "high bleached."

The Shibuya streets have spawned extreme fashions and styles before, but none quite as assaulting as the *Gonguro,* a word that literally means "blackface" in Gal language. (The first wave of browned-out girls was known as *Ganguro*, which simply alludes to a very dark, tanned face. The prefix *Gon* was added to the word as the look became increasingly hardcore.) Middle- and high-school-age Kogals had already begun darkening their skin since the early 1990s (as had hip-hop-crazed Teamer boys and urban surfing fanatics), but now the brakes were off. If the Kogals looked tan, then the Gonguro looked *burnt beyond all recognition.* Light skin had been held as a beauty ideal for centuries in Japan. But the Gonguro lived in a brave new world where one could customize anything, even skin color. So why not go all the way?

It took one person—a legendary fashion extremist named Buriteri—to take the basic idea to its next evolutionary level. In 1999 rumors began to circulate in the Shibuya underground about a girl who had created a bold new style somewhere between twisted genius and full-blown insanity. When the pioneering Gal magazine *egg* got wind of this mysterious figure, it dispatched camera crews into the discos to track her down like a wild animal.

Naming herself after the jet-black soy sauce used to flavor yellowtail fish (*buri*) in teriyaki cooking (*teri*), Buriteri was found holding court in the Shibuya club Pylon. She strutted about in colossal platform boots that made her knockout body stand nearly six feet tall, putting her literally over-the-top. Everything about her screamed "a star is born."

The *egg* staff immediately began using Buriteri in their photo spreads, promoting her as a revolutionary fashion icon for the strange new millennium to come. In public, and in the pages of *egg,* Buriteri was often seen alongside a core group of three followers who aped her style.

One of them was a girl named Yuka Mizuno. In a retrospective on the early days of the Gonguro phenomenon for *egg* magazine's book *Manba,* she recalled, "After we first became friends, we used to meet in front of First Kitchen [a hamburger joint] on Center Street. We'd just stand around and watch people go by, sometimes for as long as twenty hours at a stretch. Eventually, we decided to put a mat on the ground and sit down. We never noticed that everyone was scared of us because of the way we looked. We were too busy trading makeup secrets."

The more the girls darkened their skin, the harder it was to find skin foundation that could keep up. Luckily, Buriteri, guru that she was, had the answer: Max Factor's NW55, a type made for black women.

Buriteri never showed her face without makeup. "Even when we had a sleepover party," said Mizuno, "the only thing she would take off was her eyelashes. After a shower, she would spend two to three hours in the bathroom doing her makeup. We would bang on the door if we had to go pee." To this, Buriteri would shout back, "I am too shy to show you my real face!" She said doing herself up like that was a tool to hide her true personality. She was actually really shy and inhibited.

By 1999 *egg* was the de facto bible for gals in search of a crazy new style. Buriteri and company, who had gotten jobs as spokesmodels for a

The Gonguro San Kyodai have fun for the cameras during their 1999 prime.

Shibuya tanning salon called Blacky, became icons. They inspired a Japanese-schoolgirl arms race to create the most extreme looks imaginable. Already scandalously short skirts were hemmed even higher. Outfits were comprised solely of garish primary colors. And footwear, whether platform boots or wedge sandals, became positively gargantuan.

Blackface alone should have been social suicide, but the Gonguro were banding together and becoming a full-blown youth movement. In a 2001 sociology study, Tadahiko Kuraishi, a professor in the Department of Literature at Kokugakuin University, began a Shibuya study that attempted to dissect the rise and fall of the blackface look. In his groundbreaking work, he quotes a "Mr. Shirasugi," the owner of a store selling Hawaiian goods (popular with Gals), who accounted for the appeal: "Black music influenced the surfers, and it moved over to the dance clubs. Hip-hop culture began to influence the young and the desire to *actually become black* increased. But the most extreme forms of blackface actually originated as a kind of makeup style designed to make the girls stand out in crowded clubs and wherever else it is desired to stand out from the pack."

And, for better and for worse, that's just what the Gonguro did. Everyday folk who chanced upon them in the streets of Shibuya were shocked, outraged, and disgusted by their appearance. The media dubbed the black-faced girls *Yamanba,* a reference to an old folk tale about a hideous witch who lived in the mountains.

But even as the average Gonguro was shunned, even feared, Buriteri and her gang were becoming stars in Japan. The media called them the *Goguro San Kyodai* ("the three blackface siblings," in parody of the popular children's song "Dango San Kyodai"). Buriteri even began to appear as a regular on a daytime chat show. But the mutual love affair was short-lived.

"The media wanted to depict us as 'dirty girls,'" said Mizuno, "which was totally not true. The fact is we used to spend hours in the bathroom doing our makeup and getting ready. It took huge amounts of effort to get that look. Then there were lies that we were prostitutes, that we had AIDS. None of this was true. Because of our fashion style, none of us could find sex partners."

Two of the Goguro San Kyodai were actually college students at the time. The flak they were getting from all sides, and the need to concentrate on their studies, caused them to cease all Gonguro-related activities.

But even as the leaders of the movement went into early retirement, the blackface boom still ran rampant in the streets of Shibuya. Tanning salons, which began to spring up by the dozens during the 1998–2000 peak of the Gonguro wave, were beginning to turn away children as young as third graders.

Because of a variety of factors, *egg* magazine itself ceased publication in 2000 (it has since resumed publication). The cover shot of the then-final issue was an unforgettable image of Buriteri looking like a Barbie doll shot from a cannon and howling like a bat out of hell. After the photo session, she took the makeup off once and for all. Newspapers like the *Mainichi Daily* and magazines such as *Shukan Bunshun* reported on the dramatic makeover. Buriteri told the latter, "Rather than because of any reaction from my family, I decided to give up the Gonguro look because of how other people saw me. I'd just be sitting down somewhere and an adult would come along and point at me, screaming out stuff

like 'cockroach,' or 'How sickening!' My friends and I promised to become adults who never cared about how others felt or looked. That helped to make me really strong."

Buriteri was last seen working at a clothing boutique. Her skin coloring had since shifted to the other extreme and was snow-white.

By spring 2001, the Gonguro look was dead. A host of tanning salons, bereft of their regular clients, began to close down. The remaining salons formed an association to promote the health benefits of their services in an attempt to repair the massive damage done to their image by the Gonguro.

Buriteri as history will remember her: standing tall in Shibuya's Center Street.

But some of the Gonguro's accomplishments—such as the obliteration of the barriers between sexy and ugly, glamorous and gutter—can never be undone. ✳

Profile:

GONGURO

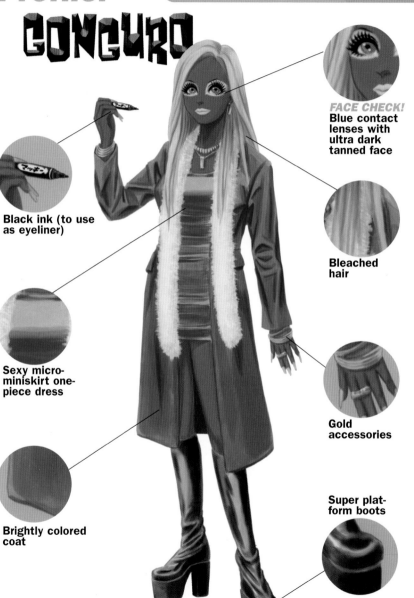

Black ink (to use as eyeliner)

Sexy micro-miniskirt one-piece dress

Brightly colored coat

FACE CHECK!
Blue contact lenses with ultra dark tanned face

Bleached hair

Gold accessories

Super plat-form boots

Ideal Boyfriend

Must Items

"High Bleach" Hair Products

Nowadays, there are plenty of colored hair extensions and other products to customize one's scalp with. But back in 2000, options were more limited. So many girls just bleached their hair themselves until it seemed to melt.

Black Skin Foundation

Imported from the United States, intended for black women.

No one! Who is going to date someone who looks like that?

Tanning Salon and Tanning Lotion
Many convenient locations in Shibuya and also throughout the Tokyo area.

Monster Platform Boots
The first Kogal boom brought thick heels back in style. The Gonguro upped the ante with boots worthy of the band KISS.

White Face Concealer
Used as lipstick.

Black Ink
Applied with an ink pen in the manner of eyeliner.

Colored Contact Lenses
Usually blue or green.

GONGURO

SEXY GALS

Gals Gone Wild
(Early 2000s to Present)

Tokyo, Shibuya, 2002

Most folks figured that after the bonkers blackface look adopted by the Gonguro died out in 2001, the girls in Shibuya were due to come back to their senses at any moment. But no.

"I keep seeing what looks like an ordinary girl, but they're all really dirty," the managing editor of a community newspaper told the Japanese culture magazine *Shukan Taishu.* "I don't know whether it's because they haven't gone home, or simply haven't had a wash. One of them was sitting on the side of the road with her panties in full view. There was an awful brown stain on them. She just sat there, staring into thin air like a zombie."

Having blown whatever money they had on clubbing, karaoke, stuffed animals, and print-club stickers, some girls decided simply to skip out on going home to Mom and Dad. They took to living on the city streets with their fellow stinky friends, dismissing basic hygiene as a total drag. As time and resources were spent in the relentless pursuit of pleasure, the girls became dropouts, not just from school but also from the rest of society to boot. What the hell were they thinking?

These fallen angels dubbed themselves *Ogals.* The *O* derived from the Japanese character for "unclean," but adding an *O* to a Japanese word can also give it a double meaning, making it honorific or cute. Ogals believed they were being both dirty *and* adorable . . . even if few outside of their permanent cloud of funk ever wanted to give them a hug.

Still, the Ogals' commitment to Being Out All the Time, no matter what, acted as a kind of natural fertilizer for a new tribe of party girls dedicated to social circles and long Shibuya nights.

Manba (the term reclaimed from the Yamanba epithet of the Gonguro) shared their black-faced sisters' fondness for tanned skin and bright, sexy clothes, but there were key differences. "The Manba like sandals better than platform boots, which can be dangerous and hard to walk in," observed an editor for the brilliantly named magazine *Ego System.* "Also, they don't get their skin tanned artificially so much, since there is a risk of skin cancer. Instead, they only wear dark-colored skin foundation." Manba favored hair extensions dyed bright pink and were crazy about supercute character-goods accessories like Hello Kitty slippers, purses in the shape of cartoon characters' faces, and key chains that resembled portable toy shops. They'd accessorize their faces with stickers of stars, rainbows, and smiley faces.

If in some ways Manba were Yamanba turned down a few notches, they cranked the volume to ear-splitting levels in their obsession with Para Para dancing to Trance and Euro-beat music.

Named after the onomatopoeic Japanese word for something falling in a wavy pattern, Para Para resembles the sort of mass synchronized hand-wringing that the Takenokozoku used to do in the streets of Harajuku in the 1980s. But being a Para Para master requires a higher learning curve. Each song spun in the clubs has specific individual moves numbering in the hundreds that must be perfectly executed. Learning the correct hand motions requires careful study of instructional DVDs (best-sellers at the HMV and Tower Records stores in Shibuya) and much practice on the part of the participants. One Para Para fanatic who

(Top) 2006's most famous Manba, Pinky, dances Para Para for a Japanese TV news show in Harajuku.

(Bottom) Kyoko Nakayama (middle) of the Gal Coordinator company promotes her business using Para Para.

Images from a typical Manba double date in Shibuya. The boys and girls adjust their hair using mirrors in a karaoke room (left) and later kill time in Tsutaya video rental shop (right).

typically practiced with friends for three to four hours in the street before hitting the clubs explained the appeal to the *Shibuya Keizai,* a newspaper that tracks economic news and trends in the area: "The group choreography of Para Para makes us feel more unified as friends."

By 2003 the guys who hovered around the clubs, feeling left out, began to imitate the Manba style (lipsticked, tanned, multicolored hair

extensions, decals on their faces, accessorized within an inch of their lives) and earned the label *Center Guy* (a play on the Japanese name for Shibuya's Center Street—*Center Gai*).

One such Center Guy confessed to the *Japan Times* in 2004, "Life for men is a real drag. We don't get to put on makeup or dress up fancy. If I could be born again, I'd want to be a girl, and work in a dress shop.

Before, when I dressed up in ordinary gear, nobody spoke to me. But when I walk down the street dressed up this way, it's easy to make friends. It's fun. You know, the only way to get girls' attention is to imitate them."

The reborn *egg* magazine, previously a must-buy item only for the girls, now began publishing *Men's egg*, which was full of hair and makeup tips for the discriminating Center Guy.

So perfectly did the sexes now mirror each other that it was sometimes hard to tell which *egg* magazine you were flipping through.

Both sexes competed for the same clothes, especially goods made by Alba Rosa and especially jackets imprinted with the Alba Rosa logo on the back. Perhaps noticing these new customers were more likely to be squatting in the streets than walking down runways while wearing its clothes, the Alba Rosa brand was less than enthusiastic about the attention. (It's said that the Alba Rosa store would actually fire staff members caught selling clothes to Manba and Center Guys.) The brand finally gave up and closed shop in 2005, promising to return once it had "cleaned up" its image.

But just as the guys were catching up with the Manba, the girls began to cut them out of the picture with an innovation that has fostered countless schoolgirl subcultures ever since. On Internet message boards accessible only via cell phones, behind closed doors, and in underage dance clubs, the Gals began to band together in ladies-only packs known as Gal Circles, or *Galsa.* Rooted in school clubs that sprang up in the 1980s, Galsa masterminded girls' nights out at the dance clubs, drinking parties (if they were of age), sightseeing trips, and even such traditional affairs as cherry-blossom viewing. Boys were allowed to tag along, but membership in the circles themselves was forbidden.

According to the *Shibuya Keizai* newspaper, 90 percent of teenage girls who came to Shibuya belonged to a Gal Circle *and* were also using Center Street as a base of operations. It speculated that there were "hundreds of circles just in the Center Street area alone. Most are made up of twenty to thirty members each." The primary meeting spots for circle members were the Lotteria hamburger joint on Center Street and the famous Hachiko dog statue at Shibuya station, the peak time was summer vacation, and the primary activity was "standing out at a club event for getting a boyfriend." Girls swarmed into the area's cafes, fast-food joints (such as

First Kitchen, known in Gal slang as "Fakkin"), video arcades, and sidewalks to set up camp. Street-fashion magazines took photos of the girls on Center Street, confirming the scene and drawing still more to the booming area.

Angeleek, the biggest Gal circle of all, and still active today, was originally created by and for Manba in 2001. Manba's roots in Gonguro (note their shared love of tanned skin), as well as the imperfect, lungfishlike evolutionary progress of one style mutating into another, are evident in the circle's official rules laid out for prospective members:

1. *You must go to a tanning salon four times a week.*
2. *You must be a devilish, strong, and* gon *[for Gonguro] gal.*
3. *You must be totally black, so black you cannot be seen in a nightclub.*
4. *You must love only Angeleek.*
5. *You must be polite.*
6. *You must not have a smelly pussy.*
7. *You must be easygoing and make a fun atmosphere.*
8. *You must be a person who has sake in your right hand.*
9. *You must be able to dance Para Para.*
10. *You must look like a gorilla.*
11. *We also welcome people with bodies like pro wrestlers.*

From the advent of the Gal Circle, the evolution of the Japanese schoolgirl fashion subculture less resembles a straight line than a many-branched tree as the Manba movement spins out new groups, including Delicer (pronounced "deli-cur," derived from *psychedelic*), trippy neohippies into scarfing semilegal magic mushrooms; Celenba, brand-obsessed girls who seek to imitate American celebrities (think Cameron Diaz); Coconba, who only collect clothes from the Cocolulu label; Romanba, who have a taste for romantic Lolita fashion; and Banba, a tribe of Gals who sought to mimic the neon pink and violet look of America's favorite doll, Barbie. ❀

Profile:

MANBA

Portable mirror

FACE CHECK!
Light-colored eye contact lenses

Alba Rosa jacket

Pink miniskirt

Plastic sheet (for sitting on the street)

White shoes

White leg warmers

Ideal Boyfriend

Must Items

Heavy Bag

Inside this overstuffed survival kit: makeup, mirrors, hair dryers, curlers, and a complete change of clothes.

Flat White Shoes

Usually dirty from standing around in the street all day.

A Center Guy, hopefully interested in Para Para and sharing some of his hair products.

Alba Rosa Clothes

Easy to spot thanks to the hibiscus flower motif. Originally designed as tropical-themed wear for urban surfers, Alba Rosa has since become the most iconic of all Manba brands. Vintage items go for top dollar on Internet auction sites.

Colored Contact Lenses

The more artificial and crazy looking the better. Purple, yellow, and oversize comic-book-character-styled pupils can be purchased without a prescription at many fashion outlets.

Face Decals

Shiny stickers of heart shapes, rainbows, cute characters, you name it. Get them at the Tokyu Hands department store in Shibuya.

Hair Extensions

The most popular color is pink. Weave in wool thread, beads, and bells for added effect.

How to: Manba Make-Up

1 Hi! I'm Yoko, an ordinary 16-year-old girl from the Shizuoka Prefecture! I'm going to show you how to do Manba make-up!

2 First, change the color of your eyes with contact lenses.

Concentrate and draw in some eyebrows.

3 Apply a thick (I mean thick!) layer of dark foundation to your face.

4

5 Using concealer, paint big white circles around your eyes.

6 Add black eye shadow.

7 Using eyeliner, draw in whatever eye shape you like.

SEXY GALS

Pajama Party (2003 to 2004)

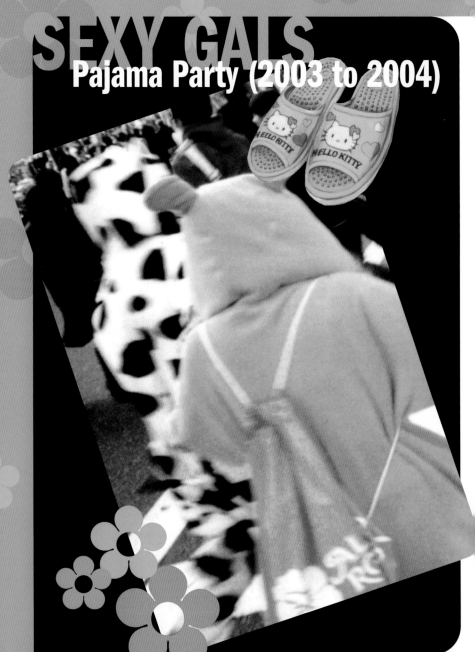

Tokyo, Shibuya, 2003

Their faces poking out from the mouths of Pikachu, Pokemon, Hamtaro, and Winnie the Pooh costumes, a group of teenage girls enthuse about their revolutionary new style to (who else?) the editors of *egg* magazine:

"One day, I just thought it would be fun to dress up in a character costume and go over to my boyfriend's house."

"I can dress like this in my local town. Anywhere. No problem. I can even sleep like this!"

"Being a Kigurumin is so much fun!"

In the wake of the Manba boom, fashions that blended cute and outrageous elements together were highly prized. But who could predict that the next look to sweep Shibuya would involve sporting cheap cloth costumes and character pajamas meant for young children?

The *Kigurumin* ("ethnic mascot" in Japanese) believed that they were creating a new species by wearing cow, bear, kangaroo, and hamster costumes while lounging in the streets at all hours. Though short-lived (lasting a little under a year, from 2003 to 2004), the Kigurumin for a time transformed Shibuya into a bizarre outdoor slumber party.

The initial inspiration seems to have come from the stinky, semihomeless Ogal, who counted dressing lazy and acting crazy among their highest virtues. The Kigurumin went one better in the comfort of cozy costumes and the always-welcome added touch of cute.

Although the Kigurumin were most often seen bumming around Shibuya, the costumes were probably first worn by Gals farther north in Tokyo's Ikebukuro District. Legend has it that a local Gal Circle, after a frenzied

Para Para dance-practice workout, sought comfortable, cheap sweat suits and jogging gear. The most convenient place to buy such items was at the Shibuya Don Quijote superstore, a kind of Wal-Mart gone wild, open 24/7 (just the place to hit after the club if you needed some plastic hair curlers, nacho dip, condoms, or a top-of-the-line Rolex). Drawn in by Don Quijote's Playboy sportswear line, the girls soon realized that the ultimate in comfort could be had by seeking out the cozy character outfits sold in the party section of the store and that wearing such comfy duds out would carry the message that they were completely at home on the streets of Shibuya.

But as with most kids on the streets of Tokyo's teen town, many Kigurumin actually lived in the suburbs. In this, they have much in common with the trashy Yanki gangs (the direct descendants of the old biker crews), who roared out of the boring badlands outside of Tokyo. They also had an unlikely, extreme taste for the cute. The toughest Yanki boy in school might be seen wearing a Betty Boop sweatshirt and cute little Hello Kitty slippers as he gulps down sickly sweet strawberry milk. He probably wouldn't want to prance around in an orange-and-black Tigger costume himself, but his girlfriend might, especially if she was feeling lazy.

After getting good ratings with Gonguro and Manba, the Gal-mad media was naturally smitten with the Kigurumin soon after they hit Shibuya. Television in particular latched onto teenage girls dressed like hamsters as the latest example of how Japanese youth had totally lost their marbles. They were shocked (shocked!) to learn that some of the girls wore nothing but bikinis under their hot plush costumes.

As 2004 rolled around and the costume-crazed gals continued to sweat it out on the Shibuya streets, Kigurumin fashion was sweeping through all

A clan of Kigurumin rush from the Shibuya train station straight into the maw of the Japanese schoolgirl inferno: Center Street.

levels of Japanese society. Television commercials and ad campaigns featured the top female idols of the day, such as Aya Ueto, dressed up as pandas. Girls wearing fuzzy cat ears became the new definition of cute for anime- and *manga*-crazed male nerds known as *otaku*. And in the sexual underground, weirdos in search of new kicks began to cross-dress as female anime characters, complete with masks, to terrifying effect, a style referred to as Dollars and Kigurumers.

The whole point of wearing wacky pajamas—to look cute and outrageous and yet still remain in a heightened state of comfort—was beginning to be co-opted by the masses. Naturally, the girls who had begun the Kigurumin look began to tire of it and decided it was time to move on. But their legacy lives on in the girls dressed like Pikachu occasionally found roaming Harajuku. They identify themselves as Decora (from the word *decoration*) rather than Kigurumin, but if the costume fits . . . ✿

Profile:

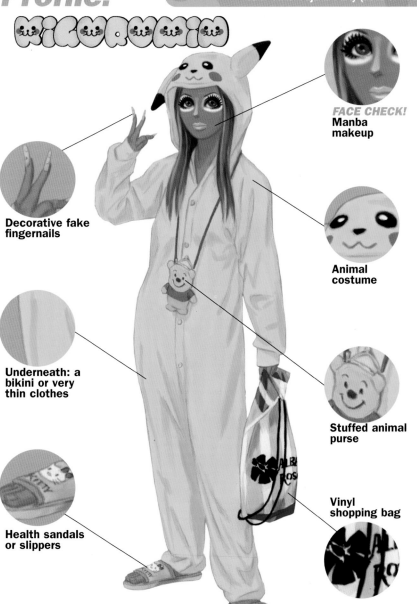

MICURUMIN

Decorative fake fingernails

Underneath: a bikini or very thin clothes

Health sandals or slippers

FACE CHECK!
Manba makeup

Animal costume

Stuffed animal purse

Vinyl shopping bag

♥ Ideal Boyfriend

Must Items

Animal Costume

Find them in the children's or party section of Don Quijote and Tokyu Hands stores.

Kigurumin are rarely seen hanging out with boys in the streets. Who wants to date a hamster?

Stuffed Animal Purse

Wallet-sized purses featuring character faces (Winnie the Pooh, especially). The Decora girls like 'em too.

Vinyl Shopping Bags

Store souvenirs from shopping sprees at name-brand stores (Alba Rosa, to name one).

Health Sandals or Slippers

Comfy shoes emblazoned with Hello Kitty or Disney characters, available at low-end department stores.

A Day in the Life: Ogal

8am

Miss last train home. Sleep in the park. Breakfast with friends (crows and stray cats).

PARCO part1
part3

Tower
Marui Record
City

10am

Carefully apply Manba makeup in front of Shibuya station.

Marui

Seibu Tokyu
HMV Department

Center Street

109-2

Shibuya109

Scramble
crossing

Hachi Dog Statue

Statue

5pm

Practice Para Para dancing in the middle of the street in preparation for yet another night of clubbing.

渋谷センター街

9pm
Coerce nasty
salesman into
buying dinner.

1am
Finally catch
the train
home. No
shower.
Pass out.

1pm
Mom says,
"Take a shower!
You two smell
awful!"

SEXY GALS
Material Girls (Present Day)

Tokyo, Shibuya, 2006

Located near Center Street, the tall, silver, cylindrical shopping complex known as Shibuya109 towers overhead. Every young woman in the area appears to be walking toward, in, or out of it. A poker-faced security guard stands watch near the door. There is a statue of a girl in a school uniform nearby, cast in bronze. Over the years, exposure to the intense Shibuya elements has turned it an onyx shade of black.

The first thing that strikes visitors to the 109 is the sound. Every store and boutique inside is blasting bangin' hip-hop and hyperactive trance music at incredible volume. The effect is like a stereo warehouse that's gone haywire or a newfangled kind of sonic weaponry. No matter where you are in the eight-story building, you have to shout over the din if you want to be heard, but it's not as if there is a lot of conversation going on inside.

Girls come to 109 to *shop,* and shop they do for the very latest in crazy shoes, shirts, dresses, underwear, swimwear, and every imaginable accessory. Customers include garden-variety schoolkids (who should probably be in class), chocolate-brown Manba tottering around on wooden sandals, ultrahip chicks in granny sweaters and strands of pearls, the terminally uncool hoping to get a rung up on the social ladder, and even the occasional transvestite or

celebrity from around the world (Paris Hilton is said to stop by 109 whenever she's in town).

Shibuya109 originally opened in 1979, and the first generation of stores inside included men's goods, a sports shop, a record store, and even a place to buy drapes. But eventually, as they did with the entire Shibuya area, the girls took it over and transformed it into a kingdom of their own. The many boutiques inside this half-crazed shopping complex—among them Love Boat, SLY, Egoist, and me Jane— now supply the customers with whatever looks they could possibly desire at prices well below those of snooty international brands.

It's been ten long years since the Kogals first began to walk the Shibuya streets in search of pricey goods and lonely old men with deep pockets. Yet the area has remained as lively as ever. The constantly changing goods inside 109 are just one reason why Shibuya continues to bring in the throngs even after the trends themselves have filed off to oblivion. The other reason is that the Gal lifestyle is a hard habit to break once you're hooked on it.

Over time, it's been OK to use the word *Gals* to describe any one of the various tribes that have come and gone, such as the Kogals, Gonguro, Manba, Ogal, and Kigurumin. The word *Gal* has simply come to mean a young woman drawn to a place like Shibuya in search of style and fashion. Perhaps only 20 percent of the customer base at 109 even sports the stereotypical tanned look. Yet most inside the 109 would be fine being referred to under the generic *Gal* label, even if the girls themselves are increasingly no longer teenagers.

Koichi Nakagawa, the editor-in-chief of *egg* magazine, explains: "What happens to those wild girls who've already gone through the most hard-core Gal lifestyles like the Gonguro? After graduating from high school, they start to tone down and begin to enter college or get a job."

But an impressive number of ex-Gals are coming back to the fold for a second helping of dressing up and acting wild well into their twenties. Says Nakagawa, "These older girls are now aiming for a sexy yet more adult look known as Onee Gal." (*Onee* means "older sister" in Japanese.)

There's already a fashion style known as Onee Kei (older sister style), but it is a bit on the conservative side and owes little to the proud and sexy Shibuya Gal tradition of excess. Instead, the Onee Gals gaze across the Pacific for inspiration, specifically to Tinseltown. More than anything, the Onee Gals imagine themselves as stylish Hollywood celebrities, à la J. Lo or Beyoncé. To this end, they deck themselves out in camouflage cargo pants, glitter T-shirts, and a veritable galaxy of glittering bling-bling accessories. There's much less Para Para dancing and bumming around on Center Street among this older crowd. Instead, the older Gals are more concerned with maintaining impossibly high social status—or at least projecting an image of it. Shopping helps.

Although the Japanese economic recession is only now showing signs of abating, the media have long been projecting desirable images of a wealthy lifestyle upon a hapless public. Good examples of the kind of celebrities that can rule the airwaves and magazine covers are Kyoko and Mika, the fabulous Kano sisters. They are a pair of plastic-surgery-enhanced middle-aged women who claim to be related to each other and who inexplicably appear on the red carpet at movie premieres (these being movies not actually starring the Kano sisters, mind you), decked out in dazzling clothes and jewels, escorted by scandalously younger men. Like Paris Hilton, they are famous, but for what exactly?

While some Gals are merely content to pretend they are ultrarich, superselfish celebrities, others are actually making the crossover. If they play their cards right, Gals can get record contracts, be the subject of photo books, and even hawk fast food. The currently reigning most-popular charisma model, Ebi-chan, can be seen in an advertising campaign for McDonald's new Ebi (shrimp) fillet burger. She's also been the spokesperson for a set of "gorgeous" MP3 players from Toshiba's Gigabeat line.

Taking their cues from such icons, the Onee Gals chase the ultrarich, superfamous look as best they can, mostly through the help of magazines like *Glamorous,* the 109 boutiques, and tiny bejeweled stickers that adorn cell phones, MP3 players, shoes, and even fingernails. But becoming a crass celebrity is only the starting point for their media-fed fantasies. At their most extreme, Onee Gals, clad in pink dresses and faux diamond tiaras, can even resemble storybook princesses.

All of these elegant superrich styles seem to have originated in the western Kansai area in Japan, specifically Kobe and Nagoya, where some girls try to resemble the daughters of rich families. The highest practitioner of this "elegant-conservative, and super girly" style is a brand called Jesus Diamante, whose lovely, pink one-piece dresses hover around the $600 range. No wonder Jesus Diamante uses a giant diamond as its corporate logo.

The high-end of the Onee Gal style is closely related to a look favored by younger women known as *Hime Gal* (Princess Gal). Although the Onee Gals would be content with walking a red carpet, the Hime Gals (clad in such pricey brands as Liz Lisa) would insist on riding up to the same event in nothing less than a glass carriage. They sport elegant pink and white one-piece dresses, tea-colored bouffant hairdos, enormous fake flowers, and big floppy pink bows. Perhaps in the process they wind up looking a bit like Stepford wives, but in their minds, the girls are the spitting image of Cinderella at the ball.

Clerks from Jesus Diamante retail stores model their employer's wares for Web site. They also keep blogs chronicling every aspect of their "gorgeous" lifestyle.

At first glance, the frilly and puffy Hime Gal look might appear to be inspired by the fantasyland Lolita fashions, but the truth could not be more different. The Lolita look evolved out of the Japanese underground scene. The Hime Gals (bless them) seem to have scant in their pretty little heads but the desire to play dress-up and look like a million bucks. If both the Hime Gals and the Lolitas seem to belong together in the same rococo painting, it's purely a weird accident of parallel evolution.

It makes perfect sense that the Gals should want to dress up like they were the matrons of a kingdom. After all, they already rule Shibuya. But there's also a restlessness that threatens to creep into their lives. After ten years of nonstop fashion evolution, where do the Gals go next?

Although we can only speculate on what will happen next, one enterprising Gal, who goes by the name of Sifow, already has an inspiring vision of the future. She calls it "Gal Revolution." ✦

Q & A

Sifow is a fast-rising young celebrity in Japan who preaches the gospel of Gal Revolution. In addition to being a recording artist, a model, and the author of an autobiography, she runs her own company, SGR, or "Sifow Gal Revolution." We interviewed Sifow in a café near Shibuya, where a baby girl stared at her the whole time with something like awe.

Q: What is Gal Revolution? What is your agenda? Is it something dangerous?

A: Over the last few years, the media have been projecting a very negative image of Gals. When I was in high school, it was the era of the Kogal. People would harass me on the train, and I'd go into a store and I could tell that people were thinking I was going to steal something.

One day I was just hanging out with my friends. We were all sharing similar experiences, and this lightbulb went off in my head. I graduated from high school in 2004, and I started thinking, what can I do to help change things? The name *Gal Revolution* just came to mind about a year later. I didn't have any idea what it was going to be, but I liked the way it sounded. At first I thought about becoming a working woman within the system. But when I'd show up at job interviews, it was clear I wasn't going to get hired. I looked too much like a stereotypical Gal. No one wants me, I figured. So I started my own company.

When I went to register the company, I wrote "Gal Revolution" in the business category. The guy working in the office said, "You can't write that; that's not a category." So I figured, I like music, so my business started out as a music company. We do event promotion, music publishing, and public relations.

Q: How many Gals in all work at the company? Are there any men on board?

A: There's around six or seven people on staff right now. Three of them are male. We are going to expand to ten people soon.

Q: *What are some of the challenges you've had to face?*

A: Well, there's still a bad image for Gals. Some of that is the Gals' fault too. We're not perfect, but we're not all bad either. But Gals get blamed for things all the time. Old men throw their cigarette butts into the street all the time, but if a Gal were standing nearby, she'd probably be blamed. What's important is that we're inspiring other Gals. They tell me, "I want to be a boss someday, too."

Q: *What's the next phase of the Gal Revolution?*

A: We're going to be opening up our own retail store inside the Shibuya109 building in May 2006. Four years from now, I'm hoping we can open our own school. The teachers would be professionals in their field, and hopefully they'd recruit the students they taught for jobs. I'd like for it to prepare Gals to work in information technology, the music industry, and entertainment.

Q: Do you have a message for the girls of the world?

A: Do whatever you can do at any given moment. Don't waste a single day. Think of something you have fun doing, and just go for it. Girls have so much power and energy, so it's easy to channel it into something else. ✦

Sifow's mini-album, *&YOU REVOLUTION*, released in February. 2006 (above).

The Gal Revolutionary herself, Sifow, being interviewed in Shibuya (left).

Profile:

FACE CHECK!
Big black
contact
lenses with
shiny dots

Hair curling
iron

Gorgeous
belt

Gorgeous
necklaces

Blinged-out
cell phone

Gorgeous
ankle
bracelet

Gorgeous
pinheel
shoes

105

♥ Ideal Boyfriend

Must items

Curling Iron

Don't leave home without it.

Decorated Fingernails

Caked in glitter and imitation precious stones. The more bling-bling they are, the better.

Gals and Onee Gals are the most popular kind of girls in Japan among guys. Any good-looking dude might feel up to the challenge, but only a super-rich man has a real chance of actually scoring with these Material Girls.

Jewel Stickers

To help image-conscious Gals make their digital cameras and cell phones look like gaudy national treasures.

Pin-Heel Shoes

Hard to walk in and easily broken, but hey, that's fashion. You can always buy more at Shibuya109.

Fake Eyelashes

The most hard-core include tiny crystals, fake diamonds, or rough bumps set between the lashes. The best-known manufacturer of such products, Shu Uemura, just opened an eyelash emporium in the Omotesando area.

Black Contact Lenses

With oversize shiny white circles inside to give off a dreamy "girls' comics" look. There are even contact lenses designed to make the eyes look like a Chihuahua's. We are not making this up.

ARTY GALS

Your Band Could Be Our Life (1980s)

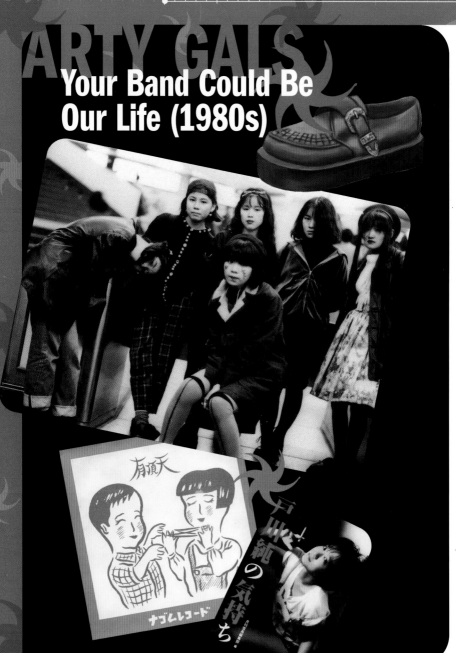

Japan, Fuji-TV, 1984

Barely twenty years old, the young woman on stage is dressed like a 1950s housewife after a nervous breakdown: polka-dot dress, black evening gloves, a big plastic flower planted on her head. A pair of silvery dragonfly wings sprouts from her back. Her name is Jun Togawa, and she is going to sing her hit song "Tamahime Sama" ("Princess Ball"), which is all about having a period.

Once a month in the corner of her cell,
Princess Ball has a stroke attack

Togawa first rose to prominence as a child actress before fronting the underground band Guernica, in the early 1980s. The turning point in her career was a series of commercials for TOTO brand toilets, featuring automated washlets (a Japanese version of the bidet), in which Togawa cheerfully chirped, "I want to wash your butt!" at the camera.

Most suspected, correctly, that Togawa was already a little "out there." But after she performed her solo number on national television in a voice that could stretch from timid little girl to soaring opera soprano in a single beat, the host of the show felt obliged to offer an explanation: "Viewers of this show, please don't misunderstand Miss Togawa. She is not a sick person. It's just that the current style of youth culture has changed."

How right he was.

Fresh-faced idol singers had long dominated the music scene, along with plenty of forgettable pop acts. Togawa (who later fronted a band called Yapoos), with her bizarre costume changes, love of the grotesque, and occasional fainting spells during performances on children's TV shows, was a revelation. She became an icon to a generation of girls who'd

never seen such powerful displays of uniquely female self-expression before.

In truth, such girls were probably weirdos themselves: class rejects, the ones who felt that they just didn't fit in with normal society or were too brainy to find contentment in simply chasing boys. Nerds or not, they searched for an alternative to the culture that was presented to them. And they found just what they were looking for in the Japanese subculture music scene.

Uchoten's *Kokoro no Tabi* (top) and *Peace* (bottom)

Girls began to gravitate toward Uchoten (Top of the World), a quirky band fronted by a guy calling himself Keralino Sandorovich, or, more commonly, just Kera. Much admired by the critics, Uchoten specialized in theatrical performances that featured interludes of sketch comedy. Their music was herky-jerky new wave, in the Devo and Talking Heads tradition. Lyrics were cynical, witty, and surreal and reveled in pointing out the absurdity of everyday life (Uchoten's song "Mississippi" admonishes listeners to brush their teeth three times a day).

Although the record-buying public at large wasn't phenomenally impressed, girls primed by the Jun Togawa experience ate it up. They snapped up Uchoten records and braved trips to music clubs where before only hard-core male music fans went to see their heroes live. Soon their field of interest expanded to include whatever else Kera, the ringleader, had to offer them.

In 1983 Kera had formed his own indie record label called Nagomu. He began scouring the underground in search of the most extreme musical acts he could find and then signing them up. The bands on the Nagomu label were vastly different from each other, and, seemed to specialize in a particular style. Among them were Tama (lo-fi folk music), Kinniku Shojo Tai (hard rock), Bachikaburi (punk), and Jinsei (from which later emerged the techno group Denki Groove).

The impressive creativity and crafty humor of the Nagomu bands not only created a devoted fan base but they also caught the attention of cutting-edge Japanese subculture publications like the comic anthology *Garo* and the magazine *Takarajima* (*Treasure Island*). *Takarajima* eventually formed a record label called Captain, which distributed Nagomu products, and in the magazine's pages, the name for the female fans first appeared: "Nagomu Gal."

The fashion sense of these Nagomu Gals covered as much stylistic ground as the acts on the Nagomu record label did. Still, some basic patterns emerged. Cool vintage clothes were highly prized. They also liked thick rubber-soled shoes (think Dr. Martens or creepers), long-sleeved T-shirts, knee-length pleated skirts, and knee-high socks. Hair could be long and straight, cut in a Louise Brooks bob, or done up in pigtails or buns with fringe bangs in the front, topped off by thick eyebrows, sometimes poking out from under a velvet beret. The favored carryall was a red or black backpack, the same one that elementary-school kids used.

A popular clothing label among some Nagomu Gals was Pink House. (Kenji Otsuki, of the Nagomu band Kinniku Shojo Tai, said in a fanzine that he liked Pink House's clothes, which is probably why many of his fans snapped them up.) The style, said to be inspired by reruns of *Little House on the Prairie,* favored ankle-length skirts, braided hairdos, straw hats, and carrying around stuffed animals (a look the Emily Temple Cute brand continues to this day). Like the Lolita years later, Nagomu Gals acted as if sexually aware womanhood were merely an option and seemed to be lost in a twisted extended childhood.

Tomo Machiyama, a former editor of *Takarajima* magazine, remembers: "They were usually short and chubby. I never once saw a tall Nagomu Gal. And they were not so cute. They were usually timid and shy, but once you got them talking, they could be very noisy and obnoxious. Maybe they were kind of like Goth girls in America, only without the darkness and the interest in sex." In truth, the Nagomu Gals weren't out to dazzle the opposite gender. The movement was more about personal expression and creativity. If they acted strange and downright loony at times, it was to mirror the image of the bands they liked.

Years later, in a 1999 interview with *Quick Japan* magazine, Kera, who started the whole scene with his label, weighed in on the relationship:

> *Most Nagomu Gals that had the stereotypical look would often say "I am not a Nagomu Gal. I don't even get along with them." I think that most of us [musicians] didn't use the term "Nagomu Gal" in the positive. Some of the band members were annoyed by their [noisy and strange] girl fans, and we had this image that Nagomu Gals were just not attractive as chicks.*

The Nagomu label shut down in 1989, but legions of Arty Girls were now loose in Japan. During the 1990s, the media came up with a new term to describe the nation's hip-but-weird chicks: Fushigi Chan (Mysterious Girls). Meanwhile, some former Nagomu Gals became creators themselves, like *manga* artists Hanako Yamada and Kiriko Nananan, columnist Kika Kayama, and the all-girl band Masako San.

The names for the scene may have changed, but the basic character type remains. But what has really altered over time is the playing field of Japanese underground culture.

Thanks to the Internet, girls looking for alternatives to the mainstream now have limitless options to latch onto, rather than just a handful of music acts on a single label, supported by a couple of must-buy magazines. It's possible that the girls who might have once fallen for the Nagomu Gal lifestyle have instead become female *otaku*: fans of mass-produced animation and comics who like to draw and write about their favorite characters. But the original Nagomu Gals prized originality when it came to fashion and style and were not content merely with imitating someone else's creations.

Instead, the true heirs to the Nagomu Gal legacy are today's arty girls in the grips of complicated relationships with gender, femininity, and the painful process of growing up: the Gothloli and the Decora. ✴

Profile:
Nagomu Gal

FACE CHECK!
Red lipstick

Sunglasses

Elementary-school bag

Long-sleeved T-shirt

Record from the Nagomu label

Knee-high socks

Thick rubber-soled shoes

Ideal Boyfriend

Must Items

Long-Sleeved T-Shirts

So long that they cover the hands. Bright colors and stripes were common.

LPs of Favorite Indie Band

Purchased in the Nishi-Shinjuku area, mostly on the Nagomu label.

筋肉少女帯

とろろの脳髄伝説

ナゴムレコード

Ideally, a member of a band on the Nagomu record label. But any indie rocker will do in a pinch.

GABA GABA HEY

Elementary-School Bag

The other option is a "can bag" designed like the classic American lunch box.

Thick Rubber-Soled Shoes

Dr. Martens and other British imports preferred.

Knee-High Socks

Or tights. Usually black, but brightly colored ones were popular too.

NAGOMU GAL

ARTY GALS

Baby, the Night Must Fall (Late 1990s to Present)

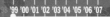

Goth White

Tokyo, Shinjuku, 2006

The menacing door at the end of the corridor is painted a bottomless shade of black. It is framed on either side by a set of human heads carved out of stone. Their mouths are covered in rusty surgical machinery, and they are screaming. Those brave enough to turn the knob and pass through to the other side will discover what looks like a mad scientist's secret laboratory, full of skulls, straitjackets, papery snakeskins, brandy snifters, broken clocks, and eerie statues that could have been shipped in from Disney's *Haunted Mansion*. As much as it resembles the set for a big-budget horror film, the spooky space is actually a boutique called Alice Auaa that sells shroudlike clothing to young women who want to look like they've just risen from their grave.

Nearby is the Moi-même-Moitié store, which is designed like a mausoleum right down to crumbling marble blocks, a padlocked gate, and enormous crucifixes that glow an unearthly shade of blue. Moi-même-Moitié sells beautiful black and white clothing that hovers around the $275 to $560 range. Adorned with lace bows and frills designed to look like something a nineteenth-century living dead doll would wear, one can complete the look with the help of spooky accessories such as gothic crosses and silver gargoyle necklaces.

Rather than in Transylvania, both establishments can be found on the fifth floor of the Marui Young shopping center in Shinjuku. It is one of the main hubs in Tokyo for the fashion that Moi-même-Moitié helpfully describes in English as "Elegant Gothic Lolita Aristocratic Vampire Romance."

If that all seems a bit dark and brooding, Marui Young is also home to a store called Baby, the Stars Shine Bright, which offers oversize bonnets and baby dresses decorated with emblems of sunny innocence and childhood like angel wings, strawberries, tasty cakes, and tiny tiaras suitable for a royal princess.

How did clothes like this, which all seem to have been magically imported from Europe circa the nineteenth century, wind up finding a dedicated following among girls in twenty-first-century Japan? And how did cute and creepy wind up becoming such good neighbors in Japan?

The roots of the Japanese Goth, and Gothloli (Gothic Lolita), scene go all the way back to pioneering late-1970s postpunk U.K. bands like Bauhaus, Sisters of Mercy, and Siouxsie and the Banshees. But the first wave of Goth only bewitched a handful of Japanese music fans, who followed the British scene and became entranced by the elaborate and decadent fashions found there. In time, the clothes proved to have more impact than the music.

A Japanese corset designer, who prefers to remain anonymous, says:

> *Gothic dress and style in Japan have only a slight linkage to the original music and club scene in the West. For instance, there are no major Goth bands or singers in Japan. It's not a popular genre among indie music fans and even fewer girls listen to it, even the ones who dress Goth. There are some monthly or seasonally Goth events that happen at nightclubs*

sometimes, but the numbers of people who go to them aren't really increasing.

Perhaps Goth style, rather than substance, won over hearts and minds in Japan because the populace lacked the cultural background necessary to really groove on stuff like rosary beads and vampire bats. Goth would have to connect with uniquely Japanese notions of darkness and doom first before it could gain momentum as a movement.

The missing link eventually turned up in Japan's own past, during the Taisho era (1912–1926), when the country was madly racing to play catch-up with the industrialized Western world after centuries of isolation. The bizarre and unbalanced mood of the times was captured in a series of obsessive and fetishistic mystery stories by author Edogawa Rampo (a pseudonym constructed to sound like "Edgar Allan Poe"). His works, among them "The Human Chair" and "The Blind Beast," helped carve out a new genre known as Ero-Guro, an abbreviation of the words *erotic* and *grotesque.* Other authors who contributed to the style include Tatsuhiko Shibusawa, Suehiro Tanemura, Shuji Terayama, and Hiroshi Aramata.

The old Ero-Guro sensibility was revived again in the 1980s as Rampo-inspired imagery started to pop up in the pages of the underground comic anthology *Garo* and subculture magazines like *Takarajima* (*Treasure Island*). Artists like Suehiro Maruo, Hideshi Hino, Keiichi Ohta, and Kazuichi Hanawa also began to infuse their work with harrowing depictions of Taisho-era sex and death, which then began to inspire others in the Japanese underground music scene to follow suit.

The first Japanese Goth bands and record labels began rising out of the mist. As with the Nagomu record label and the Nagomu Gals it inspired, fans rallied around their favorite labels. Trance Records, which had acts like YBO2, Sodom, and ZOA on its roster, boasted a heavy sound that laid down a foundation for Japanese industrial and noise rock. Its

followers, who clad themselves in all-black dress, became known as Trance Gals. The other major player in the scene was the Wechselbalg label, which, as the name implies, had a heavier European influence.

As Japanese Goth music continued to evolve into the 1990s, bands such as X Japan and Buck Tick (which seem to have their roots in the suburban Yanki scene) began experimenting more and more with their own original fashion designs. Members tried to look as distinctive as possible by applying elaborate face makeup and putting on clothes that were over-the-top hybrids of Goth and Punk.

The decade saw a huge increase in the amount of indie music being produced and distributed in Japan, resulting in an era known as the "band boom." A new generation of music acts inspired by X Japan and

A selection of (mostly) Visual Kei fans found hanging out in Harajuku in April 2006.

Buck Tick—such as GLAY, Kuro Yume, Luna Sea, L'Arc~en~Ciel—created a whole new genre called Visual Kei or Visual Style because of their eye-popping looks. The look was a hit. Sales of Western music in Japan began to dramatically decrease. As had been the case with Glam Rock and Hair Metal, androgyny was a key part of the Visual Kei aesthetic, and Japanese girls became entranced by the feminine-looking men who made the music.

While the bands fretted in front of the mirror trying to outdo each other, one act rose to the forefront: Malice Mizer. Few could ignore the band's elaborate, theatrical live shows, which invited the audience into a romantic fantasy world where decadence and innocence walked hand in hand. Malice Mizer fans were impressively hard-core and sought to replicate the fashions they saw onstage, such as the leather and lace ensembles, elaborate hairstyles, and bone-white skin pallor. And with the

right attitude and the right gear, an entire lifestyle could be constructed around an elegant and otherworldly dream.

The Nagomu Gals of the 1980s had also helped to lay down the foundation for the movement to come. Like their Gothic Lolita descendants, female Nagomu fans had a baffling air of cliquish mystery about them that tended to irritate anyone outside their circle. They also liked to make their own clothes, constructing strange fashions that toyed with a surreal vision of childhood not too far from Alice in Wonderland.

Labels like Pink House, Milk, and Emily Temple Cute first began selling gorgeous, supergirly clothes during the bubble economy of the 1980s. But the look really took off in 1988 when the Baby, the Stars Shine Bright brand was established and began to zero in on anachronistic sunbonnets and baby-doll dresses. Also adding fuel to the fire was the Vivienne Westwood label, which, around the same time, started to combine classical nineteenth-century imagery with its old U.K. punk roots.

But as the new millennium was about to roll around, girls who liked to look like antique French dolls or portraits from the rococo period by way of Goth fashions still didn't have a name for their scene. It came in the fall of 1999 when Mana, the vampiric-looking leader of the band Malice Mizer, started his own clothing brand, Moi-même-Moitié. He announced the design theme as "Elegant Gothic Lolita." Since then, the name has stuck, at least in part.

In 2001 a new magazine called *Gothic & Lolita Bible*—full of historical references, photo spreads, clothing patterns, and even features like "How to Bake a Gothic Cake"— began issuing in Japan from a company called Bauhaus. The magazine moved to another publisher, Index Communications, which was home to the cutesy-cute fashion magazine *KERA*. Both mags saw no divisions between the romantic Old World look and punk-rock staples like safety pins, combat boots, spiky dog collars, and torn fishnet stockings. It was up to the gals themselves how much they wanted to mix and match styles and eras. Naoki Matsuura, editor in chief of *KERA*, explains the connection between the media and not only the Gothloli scene but much of Japanese street fashion as well: "A lot of these girls don't

The first issue of *KEROUAC* magazine from 1998, named after the Beat legend Jack Kerouac. The title would later be shortened to *KERA*.

live in Tokyo and they have few friends in their own hometown. Magazines help create the idea that they can find a scene that they can belong to in Tokyo."

The tipping point for the rise of the Gothloli scene occurred when novelist Novala Takemono repeatedly referred to Baby, the Stars Shine Bright in his 2004 novel *Shimotsuma Monogatari,* which itself revolved around a friendship between a Lolita and a live-wire Lady's biker girl. When the book was adapted into a film later that same year (released in the United States as *Kamikaze Girls*), the Gothloli entered mass consciousness in Japan. Hence, more girls dressed like undead Marie Antoinettes than ever before, marching into Shinjuku to do their shopping, and then moving over to the nearby Harajuku District to hang out, be seen, and shop some more, usually at the Laforet shopping complex there.

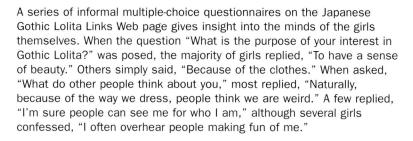

A series of informal multiple-choice questionnaires on the Japanese Gothic Lolita Links Web page gives insight into the minds of the girls themselves. When the question "What is the purpose of your interest in Gothic Lolita?" was posed, the majority of girls replied, "To have a sense of beauty." Others simply said, "Because of the clothes." When asked, "What do other people think about you," most replied, "Naturally, because of the way we dress, people think we are weird." A few replied, "I'm sure people can see me for who I am," although several girls confessed, "I often overhear people making fun of me."

Recently, Gothic Lolita imagery has started to appear in a host of animations and comics like *Doll, Le Portrait de Petit Cossette, Rozen Maiden,* and *God Child*. The style appeals to fan girls who enjoy indulging in "cosplay": dressing up as their favorite 2-D characters. The Gothloli style has now separated into two distinct groups: those who caught the bug from anime and *manga* and those who follow the Visual Kei music scene (and no, the camps don't like each other very much). In between are many different subgenres of Gothloli: the Kuro-Loli (Black Lolitas who garb themselves in a single color—guess which one?), Ama-Loli (who dress sweet and dreamy, like human birthday cakes), the Guro-Loli (who are into wrist cutting and may have serious psychological issues), Goth-Pan (punks), and Loli-Punks (as if Vladimir Nabokov could ever dream of such a thing).

As our anonymous Japanese corset maker says, "Gothloli girls don't need to fantasize about European nineteenth-century stuff any more. They have created their own fashion style, which doesn't refer to any real historical period. I wonder how many of them can tell the difference between what is nineteenth-century European and what is medieval."

Now dressing up like an extra from *Interview with the Vampire, Pollyanna,* or a punk rock mash-up of the two is a viable option for young girls in Japan. Since the style has already overcome formidable obstacles of time and space, it's possible that Gothloli could endure, like a ghost in the Tower of London, for centuries to come. After all, some respondents to the "Gothic Lolita Links" survey said, "Every girl simply wants to dress up and look cute. Lolita fashion is the tool to totally transform myself into something else." ·

Profile:
Gothloli

Parasol

Metal accessories

Doll-like shoes

FACE CHECK!
Pale skin with dark eyeliner

Frilled dress

Goth bag

Frilled knee-high socks

Ideal Boyfriend

A guy in a Visual Kei band or someone who worships at the altar of Goth and Punk music.

Headdress

(Mini Hat or Bonnet)

Both Lolitas and Gothloli alike tend to wear some kind of headdress, either a bonnet, a bow, ruffles, lace, a leprechaun-sized hat, or a headband, usually black or white.

White Skin Foundation

A pale face is a *must,* so girls keep the appropriate makeup handy. Red or black lipstick is common, but less tends to be more with the Gothloli.

Goth Goods

Mini-Me-like Goth dolls created by the Volks company. Cheaper alternatives include vampire novels and books like *Alice in Wonderland*.

Vivienne Westwood Shoes

Long the favorite choice of footwear for Lolitas and Goth kids alike.

Metal Accessories

Like something you'd use to ward off a vampire or cast an evil spell. Favorites include crosses, roses, angel wings, spiders, and butterflies. Bonus style points if they are antique.

Gothloli

11a
Take
photo
with f…
at Jing…
bridge…

12pm
Walk down
Omotesando
street near
Harajuku, feigning
innocence all
the way.

Meiji Jing…

3pm
Teatime
at a
Gothloli
cafe.

Haraju…
Static…

5pm
Savor the scary atmosphere of a Gothloli shop, then go inside.

Shinjuku Gyoen Par

9pm
Go to a Visual Kei rock show. Scream.

1am
Home at last. Change into junior high school gym suit and sew new clothes for tomorrow.

ARTY GALS

Cute Overload
(Mid-1990s to Present)

Tokyo, Harajuku, 2006

Built around the centrifuge of an old merry-go-round, the 6% Doki Doki boutique is a riot of polka-dot dresses and bejeweled accessories—brooches and bracelets designed like boo-boo kitties, clowns, and ice-cream cones. The stereo is blasting songs from Walt Disney movies. The three-girl staff, dressed like sexy circus acrobats, nod their heads in time as Kirk Douglas sings "A Whale of a Tale."

So it is today, but a decade ago, the store resembled nothing so much as a rainbow-bright explosion of American kiddy store fare (Power Puff Girls! Strawberry Shortcake!), inspiring a tribe of girls who had moved beyond playing with the dollies and figures to actually *wearing* them, becoming a walking human toy store known as a Decora (short for *decorative*). And in some ways, the Decora were the last girls to truly enjoy Harajuku in its prime as an all-access zone for youth culture and cutting-edge street fashion.

During the mid-1980s, photographer Shoichi Aoki had been regularly traveling to New York, London, and Paris to collect images for the Japanese magazine *Street*. Rather than using professional models, Aoki merely took snapshots of whatever stylish looks the locals were wearing. The Japanese fashion scene was then dominated by monochromatic colors and high-end international designers, but Aoki was unimpressed, proclaiming to the Bitslounge Web site, "I'm not someone who is interested in brands. I like to believe that true fashion is what people are wearing in the street."

In 1997 Aoki found a new inspiration closer to home. He suddenly noticed that the girls in Harajuku were dressing up in brightly colored prints and a tremendous load of accessories such as necklaces, plastic beads, and bracelets, many of which were handmade. Others were

The first issue of *FRUiTS* magazine from 1997, featuring Aki Kobayashi (right) on the cover.

inspired by the customized kimonos made by Takuya Angel, an indie label that sold its wares on the back streets of Harajuku, an area known as Ura (Japanese for "behind") Harajuku. The do-it-yourself spirit of the 1980s-era Nagomu Gal had clearly been passed on to this new breed, the Decora (or Decora-chan, to add the proper adorable diminutive).

In June 1997, Aoki was inspired to create a special issue of *Street* magazine devoted solely to these girls, who would soon ignite a style and fashion boom in Harajuku. The publication was a best seller, and a new magazine, *FRUiTS,* was created to continue Aoki's ongoing coverage of Japanese street fashion.

The name *FRUiTS* was chosen to evoke the variety of colors one finds in the natural world. The charismatic cover model of the first issue typified the emerging style. Eighteen-year-old art-student Aki Kobayashi, a fan of the charactor Sailor Moon, loved to accessorize her clothes with character goods from the show. Beginning in the third issue of *FRUiTS,* Kobayashi also began writing a column, where she described how she created her distinctive look. Her bracelets had been made out of plastic powder bought at the Tokyu Hands department store, mixed into goo, and carefully molded into the desired shapes.

Other teens followed her lead and began making similar colorful accessories and even entire brands of their own. One amateur design team was HIGE, a group of guys aged nineteen to twenty who created beautiful accessories out of wire. Naoki Matsuura, the editor in chief of *KERA* magazine, recalls the era fondly: "The girls in the late nineties had so much energy and creativity. What they were doing was more advanced than anyone working professionally in fashion and design."

Meanwhile, the Decora girls were beginning to gather on the weekends in that old haunt of the Takenokozoku, the automobile-free stretch of street known as Pedestrian Heaven. There, they bought and sold each other's arts and crafts and would occasionally get busted by the cops for doing business without a license.

While Aoki continued to stalk the area with camera in tow on a hunt for models to include in *FRUiTS* (and an Aoki imposter caused mischief throughout Japan, forcing the normally shy photographer to show his face), other magazines, such as *Zipper* and *Cutie,* also began to zero in on the Decora look and lifestyle. As ties between the publishing and fashion industries began to cement, soon there were new, more consumerist tribes of girls to choose from. They included the Cascaders, devoted fans of the band Cascade who wore colorful, fashionable clothes. The Angelers cloaked themselves in the kimono-inspired Takuya Angel gear. Then there were the Cyber kids, who brought ravelike fashions into the daytime streets. Whether their

clothes were handmade or bought off the rack, the girls were helping to push Harajuku into the middle of a full-blown fashion renaissance, the seeds of which had been planted a few years earlier.

In 1995 a young couple opened a store, 6% Doki Doki, in the "cat street" back alleys of Ura-Harajuku. Emiko Saito and "Sebastian" (not his real name) were deep into avant-garde art and theater, and they occasionally helped out the famed Shuji Terayama when he put on productions. But the underground scene was not their only inspiration. Says Sebastian, in an official statement on the 6% Doki Doki Web site, "We also went to techno clubs where people used to wear a lot of accessories."

Saito remembers, "We called our store 6% Doki Doki [a Japanese word for the sound of a heart beating fast] because we just wanted to add just a little extra bit of excitement to people's lives."

The stated concept behind 6% Doki Doki was "sensational lovely." The owners stocked overpowering amounts of cute character goods and cheap toys, many of them imported from America. The store was

designed to look like a psychedelic garden of giant Day-Glo magic mushrooms. Says Saito, "We wanted go beyond cute and try to cross over into the kind of funny bad taste that old ladies sometimes have."

As Harajuku began to heat up, some very big fish began to visit the store. Remembers Sebastian in the official store history, "Sofia Coppola visited once, and it was covered by *H* magazine. Things started to get really crazy after that." Other celebrities began dropping in, including members of the band the Boredoms and a TV personality named Tomoe Shinohara.

A frequent guest on talk shows, Shinohara was the missing link between Nagomu Gals and the new Decora generation. A Cyndi Lauper–like figure who dressed like a little girl, talked loudly, and was high spirited bordering on obnoxious, she also made her own accessories and released several records of electronic pop music. Also seemingly cut from the 6% Doki Doki cloth were Ai Kago and Nozomi Tsuji, two very young members of the girl-group Morning Musume who looked every bit like two Decora youngsters pulled right off the Harajuku back streets.

But, says Saito, "Because of all the media attention and the kids all wanting to get in the magazines, it purely became a competition to see how outrageous you could look. I began to feel like something had gone really wrong. Our customers weren't interested in art and literature like we were. They only wanted to look fashionable and stay empty inside."

It was an old story, the same one that had provided the fuel for other extreme fashions and trends such as Ganguro. Back home, the Decora were faceless nobodies. Being plucked out of the street to have a picture taken for a magazine held the promise of an "I am somebody" moment of redemption. The rush had to be obtained at any price.

"I only wanted the customers to feel 6 percent excitement, but they wanted 100 percent," muses Saito. "When the girls started doing crazy diets and taking drugs to lose weight, I figured that I'd had enough."

Saito moved to San Francisco, where she is now a massage therapist. Sebastian stayed behind and continues to run a somewhat differently styled 6% Doki Doki (think Circus Circus meets Frederick's of Hollywood).

Just as the Harajuku street-fashion scene was beginning to attract international attention, the rug was rudely pulled out from underneath. In 1998 the decades-long tradition of closing down the streets to automotive traffic came to an end at the behest of the Tokyo Metropolitan Government. Said photographer Aoki to the Bitslounge Web site, "It really caused the energy to go down. It's sad

(Top left) A pair of Decora arrive in Harajuku dressed as Pikachu. Both are fourteen years old and are from the Tokyo suburbs.

(Bottom right) More Decora dressed in cozy costumes invade Harajuku for the weekend.

that the place that created so many new kinds of Japanese fashion was violently taken away during its peak."

And yet, the myth of Harajuku as a still-buzzing fashion mecca endures today even as the fashion styles have turned to ho-hum hip-hop gear and punk without the politics. Tourists come from all over the world hoping to get a glimpse of the famed "Harajuku Girls" that Gwen Stefani once sang about. The magazine photographers are still there at the street crossings hoping to catch a new style in the bud, but the colors and creatively have visibly dimmed. Most of the excitement is farther up the street at Omotesando Hills, a shopping mall of international brands that resembles nothing so much as duty-free stores at an airport.

Meanwhile, all that remains of Harajuku's once-massive Pedestrian Heaven is a mere crossing bridge where maybe fifty kids, at best, gather on the weekends. Alongside the Lolitas, the punks, and the tourists there, you'll sometimes see a Decora, decked out in cheap bracelets and a daffy polka-dot print dress like in the old days.

Let's hope the various tribes put their heads together and come up with something new soon. ♥

Profile: Decora

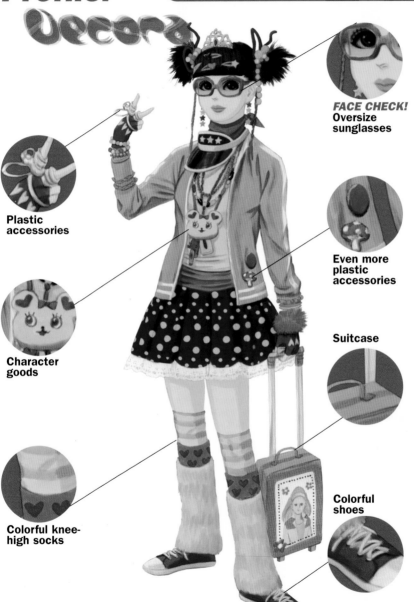

Plastic accessories

Character goods

Colorful knee-high socks

FACE CHECK!
Oversize sunglasses

Even more plastic accessories

Suitcase

Colorful shoes

Ideal Boyfrien

Must Items

Character Goods

Purses, key chains, and even figures bought from 6% Doki Doki or elsewhere. The most popular are Winnie the Pooh; Marie, from Disney's *Aristocats;* and Hello Kitty.

Plastic Accessories

Handmade wire accessories were popular until 2000, but now tastes have shifted to colorful and toylike hoops, rings, necklaces, and earrings.

A creative sort, perhaps more than a little childish, who likes hanging out in the streets of Harajuku in brightly colored gear. Bonus points if he's willing to share some of his character goods, too.

Suitcase

Rolling child-sized carryall to put clothes and accessories in for a quick change or for trading with friends.

Flared Skirt

In the same Rainbow Brite tradition as the socks. Multiples are worn to get the layered look.

Colorful Knee-High Socks

Worn in multiple layers.

What Kind of GAL Are You?

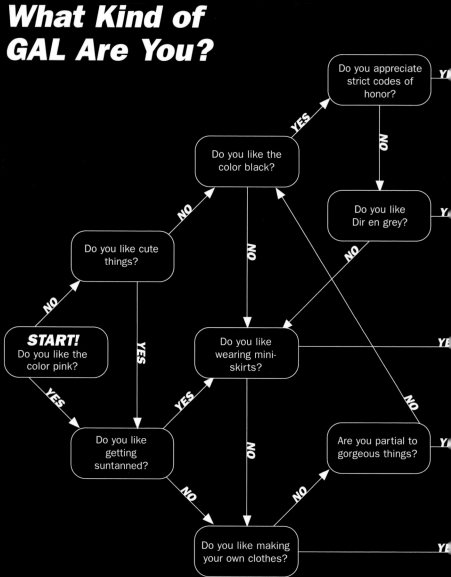

Do you appreciate strict codes of honor?

Do you like the color black?

Do you like Dir en grey?

Do you like cute things?

START!
Do you like the color pink?

Do you like wearing mini-skirts?

Do you like getting suntanned?

Are you partial to gorgeous things?

Do you like making your own clothes?

Note: If you end up just going around in a loop while taking this questionnaire, you are not yet suitable to fit in with one of the tribes.

ARTY GAL

Gothic and Lolita gear could be your most suitable clothes. Amazingly, you can get them in Tokyo now without having to travel back to the 18th century.

Gothloli Buy your wares at small shops in such Tokyo hoods as Harajuku, Shibuya, and Daikanyama. Shinjuku's Marui Young shopping center also has lots of Gothloli stores.

Gothic Lolita Links (Japanese only)
www.gll.jp

SEXY GAL

You are a party girl and love to stand out in crowd. Now it's time for you to take a big step: Manba makeup!

Manba Tokyo's Shibuya district is the mecca of Manba style of fashion. The Shibuya109 building is a good place to compete with other super-tanned girls for clothes and accessories.

Gal Fashion Community
www.ricoche.net

SEXY GAL

You are probably in high demand among the guys. You love being a girl and know how to make the most out of it.

Gal Japanese women's fashion magazines like *CanCam* and *JJ* are the bible of today's trendy styles. But if you like the classic Kogal style, stick to *egg* magazine.

Sifow's site (Japanese only)
www.sifow.net

Harajuku is the

Photo Credits

Acknowledgments

Special Thanks

Shiho Fujita and Hiromi Nishimoto
(Sifow Gal Revolution)

Nobuaki Higa (*Teen's Road*
magazine)

Mamiko Hosoya

Emiko Keduka

Miwa Komatsu

Miho Kondoh

Tomohiro Machiyama

Naoki Matsuura (*KERA* magazine)

Shunichi Miura (ex-Uchoten)

Junko Mizuno

Koichi Nakagawa (*egg* magazine)

Junichi Nakajima (Bamboo Memory:
www.geocities.jp/marubina/index.htm)

Kyoko Nakayama (GAL Coordinator)

Emiko Saito

Ryo Tochinai

Makiko Yanagi

Ayako Akazawa

Steve Mockus

Beth Steiner

cu.
5. 1
Evers,

TT562.M
305.235'20

2006024947

Manufactured in China

Designed by Izumi Evers

Distributed in Canada by Raincoast Books
9050 Shaughnessy Street
Vancouver, British Columbia V6P 6E5

10 9 8 7 6 5 4 3 2 1

Chronicle Books LLC
680 Second Street
San Francisco, California 94107
www.chroniclebooks.com